DATE			

IS MY HUSBAND GAY, STRAIGHT, OR BI?

IS MY HUSBAND GAY, STRAIGHT, OR BI?

A Guide for Women Concerned about Their Men

Joe Kort, PhD
With Alexander P. Morgan, PhD

ROWMAN & LITTLEFIELD
Lanham • Boulder • New York • London

Published by Rowman & Littlefield
A wholly owned subsidiary of The Rowman & Littlefield Publishing Group, Inc.
4501 Forbes Boulevard, Suite 200, Lanham, Maryland 20706
www.rowman.com

16 Carlisle Street, London W1D 3BT, United Kingdom

British Library Cataloguing in Publication Information Available

Library of Congress Cataloging-in-Publication Data

Kort, Joe.
Is my husband gay, straight, or bi? : a guide for women concerned about their men / Joe Kort, with
Alexander P. Morgan.
pages cm
Includes bibliographical references and index.
ISBN 978-1-4422-2325-7 (cloth : alk. paper)—ISBN 978-1-4422-2326-4 (electronic)
1. Husbands—Sexual behavior. 2. Sexual orientation. 3. Bisexuality. 4. Homosexuality. 5. Sex in
marriage. I. Morgan, Alexander P. II. Title.
HQ1035.K67 2014
306.872'2—dc23
2014007515

Printed in the United States of America

DISCLAIMER

The case stories presented in this book are based on my thirty years of experience as a psychotherapist and sexologist, but none of them represents an actual case. The characters and situations are composites created to enhance clarity and ensure anonymity. If it appears that a real person is being described, this is entirely coincidental. No real person is being referred to or described in these pages.

For my professional colleagues: In this book, we consider a variety of fetishes, partialisms, and paraphilias and discuss them as needed. However, I have generally chosen not to use these clinical terms to avoid an unnecessarily complex range of clinical definitions and terminology. Instead, I use the catchall term "kink" to include all atypical sexual behaviors and interests. In chapter 12, I do briefly discuss paraphilias, but, generally, I use "kink" where I would use fetish, partialism, paraphilia, and so forth in a more clinical book.

This work is dedicated to all the straight men
who have taught me about the fluidity of male sexuality.
You were honest and brave.
You faced skepticism and scorn.
I can do no more than be inspired by your example.

I appreciate your insistence, but no, I'm not gay.

—Eric Barry

CONTENTS

ACKNOWLEDGMENTS

The first person I'd like to thank is my husband, Mike Cramer, who has supported all of my writing endeavors and pretty much anything else I wanted to do. You have encouraged me to grow. You have fueled my thinking for my professional work as well as in my personal life. I am eternally grateful to you.

Clinical psychologist David Ley was very helpful in his comments on chapter 3 and offered a number of useful perspectives on "cuckolding." I am in awe of your wisdom and intelligence. You have helped me think differently on many aspects of sexuality, and I am grateful to you and your writings.

Sex therapists Neil Cannon and Tamara Pincus read a preliminary version of chapter 5 and offered a variety of insights on BDSM and the BDSM community. Your feedback was invaluable. Thank you.

I want to thank my sister, Lisa, and her four children—Jacob, Zack, Noah, and Zoe—for being the playful part of my life. My breaks from writing and other professional endeavors have included our adventures such as going to movies, shopping, sleepovers, and trips. You've helped me remember what life is all about and renewed me to come back to work on this book.

I also want to thank those who disagreed with me that straight men can have sex with men and not be gay (or bisexual). Every challenge, every debate, every criticism, and every argument has helped clarify and strengthen my understanding of this surprising reality. It is the truth, and it deserves to be understood and recognized.

And, finally, I would like to thank Alexander Morgan, who believed in this topic and agreed to help me give my ideas and thoughts a voice by writing this book with me. We certainly learned a lot as we struggled with terminology and ideas that were hard to describe in words. The challenges we faced while writing make this book all the better. Thanks for your inspiration in writing with me and transforming my thoughts into beautiful words.

* * *

Alexander would like to thank Susan Schwartz for helpful suggestions to improve the proposal for this book while it was in early stages of development. He wants to thank, with love, his wife, Janice, whose support was, as always, invaluable. Finally, he would like to thank Dr. Joe Kort for allowing him to go along on the journey of this book. It's been an adventure. It's been fun.

* * *

We both would like to thank Suzanne Staszak-Silva at Rowman & Littlefield for her prompt and cheerful responses to all our questions.

PREFACE

Your Husband Probably Isn't Gay

Jennifer can't believe it. Just married and pregnant, she discovers that her husband has been meeting Brad for sex. When confronted, Tom doesn't deny it, but he insists it's just "a thing" and he isn't gay. Jennifer is sure her marriage can't survive, but things are not as bad as she fears. After seeing me for therapy, Tom and Jennifer come to understand that even though some of Tom's sexual behavior is gay, his sexual orientation is straight. His compulsion to have sex with men is rooted in the abuse he suffered as a boy from a school coach. Therapy gives him relief. Tom and Jennifer are able to repair their relationship, reestablish trust, and save their marriage.

John's wife, Karen, is just as upset as Jennifer was when she discovers that her husband likes to watch gay porn. In my office, Karen raises the same questions that Jennifer has: *Does this mean my husband is gay? Can my marriage survive?* After a period of therapy, I determine that John is, in fact, not gay. Although therapy can diminish a man's dependence on fantasies and porn, sometimes the simplest and most effective "solution" is not to worry so much about it. After Karen understands that John's interest in gay porn isn't a threat to her marriage, she becomes less concerned, and the "crisis" is partly resolved by acceptance.

Tom wants sex with men, although he isn't gay. John watches gay porn, but he also is not gay. Their stories illustrate the fact that men can be straight but have gay sexual interests. The distinction between gay men and straight men with gay interests is significant. Straight men generally can make their marriages to women successful. Gay men often cannot. Bisexual men are somewhere in between. One of the purposes of this book is to explain the best relationship options for these three types of men.

Women are increasingly concerned that their men might be gay. Television and books warn of "gay husbands" who endanger their wives by having unprotected sex with AIDS-infected strangers. Politicians and celebrities are forced "out," and their wives tell the press they "had no idea." Thanks to the Internet, straight men with gay sexual fantasies now easily find partners to act them out. Men who seek more and more purely sexual experiences discover they can turn to men, not out of a gay orientation but because often men are more easily available than women for casual sex.

Recent studies have confirmed a trend to blur the boundary between gay and straight. According to the *New York Times*, "the fastest-growing group along the sexuality continuum are men who self-identify as 'mostly straight' as opposed to labels like 'straight,' 'gay' or 'bisexual.'"[1] This trend away from a rigid interpretation of sexual orientation is also the focus of Lisa Diamond's book, *Sexual Fluidity*.[2]

Psychotherapist Ian Kerner, whose books have been best sellers—for example, *She Comes First: The Thinking Man's Guide to Pleasuring a Woman*[3]—told me recently: "Lots of women in New York City, at one time or another, have wondered if their boyfriends might be gay. It's a topic I'm often asked about when I give a talk to the public."[4]

The *New York Times* confirmed this concern by women in an article published on December 7, 2013: "In the United States, of all Google searches that begin 'Is my husband . . . ,' the most common word to follow is 'gay.' 'Gay' is 10 percent more common in such searches than the second-place word, 'cheating.' It is 8 times more common than 'an alcoholic' and 10 times more common than 'depressed.'"[5]

Why would a straight man be drawn to gay sex? The reasons are many, including sexual opportunism, sex addiction, and sex for money, but the most common reason is trouble in the man's childhood involving a male sexual abuser or other assaults to the boy's masculinity. These attacks on the child generate guilt and shame, which carry over to adulthood. They embed in the man's psyche as sexual fantasies, which the man often feels compelled to act out. This "eroticizing of childhood trauma" happens even if the early trouble is not sexual abuse. By investigating a troubled client's "core sexual scripts," that is, his most compelling sexual fantasies, a therapist can uncover what happened in the past and work with the client to lessen the force of his compulsions. Therapy will also help to diminish the crippling effects of chronic guilt and shame in other areas of a client's life that are common consequences of severe trouble in childhood.

You may be better able to sympathize with the sexual issues of your man when you understand what is driving his behavior. As long as the spotlight is on kinky sex fantasies and behaviors, you may find it difficult to feel empathy. When the focus changes to childhood abuse, you can then find a window to understanding and healing.

But wait. A man's sexual interests may appear to be "gay sex" without being gay at all. Many sexual kinks are interpreted by both wives and husbands as "gay behaviors." That happens particularly because our homophobic society tends to make people hypervigilant about "men who act gay." The man's kinks may require some therapy or at least better communication and less secrecy, but he isn't gay just because he has some atypical sexual interests.

A Google search for "gay husband" or "straight men who have sex with men" hits hundreds of thousands of sites, but the information there is often unclear, imprecise, or wrong. Few bloggers are legitimate therapists. Trauma-driven sexual compulsions are commonly confused with a gay orientation, as are many kinks and unconventional sexual behaviors. This book will give you clear, concise, and accurate information, unlike what you might get from a Google search.

I have been a licensed psychotherapist for thirty years, and in that time I've helped many couples stay together when "gay panic" seemed to be breaking them apart. Because I am gay and an authority on issues of sexual orientation, I have often been called in to help such couples; and based on my experiences with them, I have been motivated to write this book about men who seem to have gay interests who are not gay and can remain happily married to an informed woman.

I have also been one of the pioneering psychotherapists to understand the therapeutic usefulness of clarifying and "decoding" the core sexual scripts of a man who is straight and troubled by gay sexual fantasies. Understanding how these scripts work is an invaluable insight for wives and husbands struggling to save their marriages.

Is My Husband Gay, Straight, or Bi? is a psychological self-help book, similar in purpose to Harville Hendrix's *Getting the Love You Want: A Guide for Couples*.[6] Like that best seller, this book is intended to help couples when the partners must deal with psychological issues left over from childhood; but unlike Hendrix's book, the focus here is on straight male partners who seem to be drawn to gay sex.

Marriages can be hurriedly terminated because men and women (and their therapists) lack the information they need to understand a couple's true options. This book provides clarity, describes options, and (in many cases) offers hope for relationships and marriages that, in the past, might have been abandoned. *Is My Husband Gay, Straight, or Bi?* is a unique and valuable resource for couples and their therapists.

* * *

This book is divided into two parts. Part I considers the lives of men and women struggling with the impact on their relationship of the man's sexual behavior. Either he is drawn to sex with men, or he has sexual impulses that seem to be gay. The stories in these chapters illustrate the very different situations you might be facing.

Part II takes a broader perspective. Chapters 10–12 offer general insights and understandings about the types of men whose issues are illustrated by the stories in part I. Chapters 13–15 give options for various kinds of actions you might take, depending on what you are dealing with. Chapter 16 briefly describes a variety of other situations in which straight men will seek sex with men, and chapter 17 sums it all up. The appendix is a guide to therapy. The bibliography includes books, articles, and websites that provide further resources and support.

I

What Is Happening?

I

JENNIFER'S CONUNDRUM

Straight Men Who Want Sex with Men

Sometimes life hits you in the head with a brick.

—Steve Jobs[1]

Jennifer felt the pieces of her life coming together at last. She and Tom had held off getting married while they waited to see if he would keep his job. So many engineers were being laid off, especially in the auto industry. But now, all at once it seemed: the industry was looking up, they got married, Tom was offered his long-delayed promotion, and she had gotten pregnant on their honeymoon in Hawaii. Jennifer was the happiest she'd ever been in her thirty-two years on earth.

Tom's promotion meant that they'd be moving from Warren to Ann Arbor. Both communities were in the Detroit area, but Tom felt Ann Arbor was too far from Warren to commute. The move was disorienting but not unexpected. A kindergarten teacher in Warren for the past ten years, Jennifer felt hopeful she'd be able to find a similar job in Ann Arbor. Now, they were hurriedly packing. Tom was scheduled to begin his new position in a few days. Jennifer hadn't even had time to let her principal know she'd be leaving.

Her cell phone started ringing. It was Tom. "Hi, hon," he said. He was at work, his last day at the Warren office. "There's a file I can't find on my computer here," he said. "Can you check to see if it's on my desktop there?"

"Just a minute." She went to his home office. She turned on the floor lamp and pushed "shift" on the keyboard to wake his computer. "It wants a password," she told him.

"Just hit enter, hon. There really isn't a password."

She did, and his computer jumped to display his favorite picture of her, the one from the beach in Hawaii with her laughing, holding her sunhat on with one hand and adjusting the top of her bikini with the other.

"Look in 'Work Documents,'" he was saying. "It's called 'New Proposal.'"

"I see it," she said.

"That's a relief. Thought maybe I deleted it or something. Okay. Thanks. Be home late probably. Got to finish here. Love you." And he hung up.

He worked late a lot, but that's the way it was these days, with everybody wanting to prove they weren't candidates for the next wave of layoffs. But he was doing fine. The company liked him. He was being promoted. She noticed a folder with a funny name. "Craigslist Sales," it said. *Oh*, Jennifer thought, *I didn't know he was selling stuff on Craigslist.* She opened it. The files inside were named with what seemed to be dates. She opened 070511. It began, "Bi curious? Meet to talk and maybe more." And there was contact information. Jennifer couldn't believe what she was reading. She opened another. "Find gay, bi, curious guys for free near you with Grindr on your iPhone." She opened others. They were all like that.

She hated herself for doing it, but she went into his e-mail. It didn't take her long to find what she didn't want to find. "Can't stop thinking how great you are," the most recent message said. "Sorry couldn't make it last week, but can meet you today at the usual place anytime after 5:00." It was signed, "Your alpha top, Brad." It was dated yesterday.

Jennifer was waiting for Tom when he got home that night at eight. She had printed out all the files in the "Craigslist Sales" folder. She had printed out all the e-mails from Brad. She sat in the living room, hugging these papers to her chest as if they were a comfort rather than a torment. She had been crying for hours, but now she was all cried out.

Tom's usual "What's for supper?" greeting died on his lips when he saw her sitting, red-eyed with her mouth a grim hard line. Instead, he asked, "What's wrong?"

"This," she replied, and threw the papers at him. He picked up one sheet and glanced at it, lost his easy smile, and sat down across from her.

"I was going to tell you," he said. "I didn't mean to be sneaking around."

"Tell me what? That you're gay? That you're going to leave me? That you're going to take me to Ann Arbor, where I'll be pregnant and jobless, and dump me there?"

Tom looked stricken. "Of course not. I'm not gay. I love you. We're going to have a child, a family . . ."

"You're not gay? You've been seeing this Brad character. Having an affair. You've been having sex with him."

"No," Tom said. "I did meet with him, but we didn't have sex."

"That's not what these e-mails say."

"We did some stuff together," Tom admitted, "more like . . ." He was actually trembling. "It was just. . . . I needed to. . . . It's just a thing. It's about sex, I guess, but we didn't have sex. Not really."

"You can't put me at risk like this," Jennifer said. She was suddenly calm, methodical. "Tell me exactly what you did with Brad and what's going on here."

JENNIFER'S OPTIONS

She first came to see me a few weeks after her confrontation with Tom. She told me about the e-mails and even brought copies to show me.

"He says he's not gay," she said, and her words dripped with skepticism. "He says it wasn't sex. It was just 'fooling around.' What kind of stupid does he think I am? He says he loves me and doesn't want to leave me. How can I believe a word he says? He's been lying to me. He's been having an affair . . . with a man."

"I hear you're angry."

"Of course I'm angry," she glared at me, then looked down. "I'm devastated. I was so happy. We wanted children. I'm pregnant. I told you that? It all seemed so perfect."

"And now?" I waited, but she didn't go on. I prompted her. "I hear you're afraid Tom's gay. He's going to leave you. What does he say about that?"

"He says he loves me, wants to stay married, make a family. But how can he want me and . . . Brad? It doesn't make sense."

"So, you think he's not telling the truth?"

"He's never been a liar," Jennifer admitted. "I think he's confused. Soon he'll realize he's gay, and then that will be that, and I'll be left with a baby and no husband. I was going to quit my job and go to Ann Arbor." Her voice turned hard. "I refused to go with him. He's there, but I won't go . . . not until we figure this out. My friends tell me to cut my losses, leave him since he's going to leave me. And *not* quit my job. Get ready to take care of myself and my baby."

"He could be telling the truth," I said. "He probably is confused, but he might not be gay. You might be able to save your marriage."

She fixed me with her schoolteacher no-nonsense look. "Can you explain that?" she asked.

"If a man has a gay identity . . . if he's born gay . . . then to feel right about himself he needs to socialize with other gay men. He's turned on by men. He imagines the comforts of making a home with a male partner, and, yes, he's most inclined to express his sexuality with another man. He has a gay identity. His erotic responses are gay. He's romantically gay. His sexual fantasies and behaviors are gay.

"This last part, the sex part, is not enough to make a man gay. Straight men—that is, men who are naturally most comfortable in romantic and sexual relationships with women—are sometimes drawn to . . . or even feel a compulsion to . . . fantasize about or have sex with men."

"I'm not sure I understand what you're saying."

"It is confusing, isn't it?"

"It's more than confusing," she said. She gave me a sad smile. "It's a conundrum."

"It can seem that way, but we can sort it out. Do you think I could talk with Tom?"

"I guess he'd do that."

"I'll ask him some questions. Things may not be as bad as you think."

BEYOND SEX AND ROMANCE

Tom might be a straight man who is drawn to have sex with men, or he might be gay. What's the difference, and why does it matter to Jennifer's marriage?

What it means to be gay is misunderstood by almost everyone. This is partly because of the confusion caused by political and religious prejudices, but it is also because the human body-and-soul partnership is complex and subtle and difficult to understand, even by honest and unbiased investigators. What does it mean for a man to be gay?

The answer to this question is important if you're a woman connected to a man who is drawn to have sex with men. If your man is gay, then it is going to be difficult for you to have a functional marriage. Not impossible, but difficult. (See chapter 13 on mixed-orientation marriages.) On the other hand, if he is not gay, then that's not the case. If he's not gay, and he and you want to have a marriage that works, then the chances are you can.

Some men are straight, some are gay, and some are in between. I'm going to spend some time describing "gay" now, and we'll consider the others later.

No one thing that a man does makes him gay. It's important to keep this in mind.

> No one thing that a man does makes him gay.

To be gay, a man must have gay sexual fantasies and be drawn to gay sexual behaviors; demonstrate a gay erotic desire; have gay romantic hopes, dreams, and behaviors; and have a gay identity. Each of these four aspects involves a set of behaviors and needs. A gay man will be strongly and consistently gay in these four related but different ways.

> A gay man has enduring gay sexual fantasies and behaviors, demonstrates a consistent gay erotic desire, is always romantically gay, and has a gay identity.

Let's consider each of them. Having gay sexual fantasies or behaviors means imagining sex between men or engaging in sex between men. It should not be necessary to list which acts are sexual and which are not, but many people make arbitrary and illogical distinctions, partly because of legal, moral, or religious considerations. Let's agree that "sex" includes any sort of sexual activity with the understanding that we have not tried here to clarify such things as the difference between a sexual kiss and a nonsexual one.

What is "gay erotic desire"? Imagine a man is walking on the beach. Scantily clad people of both genders are there. Whom does he notice? A gay man will notice the men. The women might as well not be there. (A straight man will notice the women and not see the men.) This reaction is deeply programmed. It's as if a gay man's sexual soul is wired directly to his eyes, and unless he is resisting or directing himself to some purpose—such as, say, he's a policeman and he's on the lookout for a female criminal—the men will overwhelm his visual circuits. He can't help it. It's automatic. This "beach test" is telling for gay men and for straight men, because a man's sexuality is strongly visual.

One variant of the beach test is "youthful noticing." A gay man often will tell me that as a prepubescent boy, he was noticing with pleasure other boys his age, often without any sense that this noticing was sexual or romantic. Straight men never tell me this.

A man's sexual orientation is strongly indicated by the beach test.

Let's pause here, so I can go on the record about something: As I describe various characteristics of the aspects of gayness, it may sometimes sound like an uncomfortable echo of the cruel homophobic game of "catching" someone who is gay by his "non-masculine" appearance or behavior. Not that gay men tend to be particularly non-masculine, but that's the prejudice. There is nothing wrong with being gay. I am happily gay myself. It is also okay to be a straight man with soft or "feminine" characteristics, behaviors, or interests. As we differentiate straight from gay and in between, as we consider various aspects and characteristics, ultimately only the man himself can decide if he is gay. Although he should usually inform the people close to him, for his sake as well as theirs, and try not to make false promises or tell lies, his sexual orientation is fundamentally his business and not the business of nosy or nasty strangers.

Sometimes a man who is essentially straight has a compulsion to fantasize about, watch porn about, or act out sex scenes with men. A common reason for this is that he has experienced certain kinds of childhood abuse or neglect. (We'll look at other reasons, too, in chapter 16.) When a straight male client tells me he has a history of compulsively and repeatedly acting out specific sexual scenarios with other men, I expect to discover in therapy that he was (for example) sexually abused by a male relative, teacher, or priest. The repetitive compulsion is caused by my client's need to "overcome" the bad feelings from his abuse. (This development of "core sexual scripts" from abuse or neglect is explained in detail in chapter 11.) Usually, with therapy, the force of the compulsion can be diminished or eliminated. I've also had male clients compulsively and repeatedly seek the comforting arms of men, and they will trade sex for this comfort. A "father hunger"—we discover in therapy—is often driven by extreme childhood neglect, and again the force of the compulsion can be diminished through therapy. Although therapy allows these men to reclaim control over their lives and have successful marriages, the urge of the acting-out behaviors or fantasies rarely goes away entirely. It is deeply encoded in their psyches.

A gay man who is not a victim of such childhood abuse has the desire to express his sexuality with men but not in a compulsive way. He may sometimes be interested in a quick sex act with little personal interaction, but he is also capable of appreciating and enjoying a male partner in more full and loving ways. He thinks men are wonderful. He is capable of gay romance.

We all know what romance is. You hold hands. You look goofy-eyed at your lover, and he looks goofy-eyed back. You kiss. You fantasize about the house you'll furnish together, the trip to Paris you'll take together, the way you'll grow old together. You want a partner who cuddles you in the morning, calls you at noon just to say "I love you," and tells you over supper what you are thinking before you say it yourself. A typical gay man—at least, if he's given a chance to become comfortable with his gayness and a few years to transition through "gay adolescence"—will long to find a partner he can be romantic with. He will brave the stormy seas of romantic thrills and heartaches seeking a man to be the love of his life. Straight men do not do this with men. The tendency of gay men to develop their gay romantic side is natural for them, but straight men, even straight men who have sought sexual relations with men, even straight men who have tried to live a gay life, never do.

Beyond sex, desire, and romance is the deep and important mystery of identity. We all understand identity at some level. We identify with our family, the schools we've attended, our country, our religion, our ethnic origins. "I am one of those Smiths." "I'm a Bulldog." "I'm a Polish American." But as important as these and other cultural and racial identifications can be, deeper and more important is our *sexual identity*, also called *sexual orientation*. That word "sexual" is misleading. A person's sexual identity is not just about sex. It is more like a tribal identity than a signifier of sexual preferences. An honest celibate gay priest has no sex life, or romantic life either, but he knows he's gay.

> A person's sexual identity is not just about sex.

IS YOUR MAN GAY?

I will summarize here some of the key observations I make when a man comes to me confused and questioning his sexual identity. Although what follows is fairly straightforward, it is sometimes difficult for men to know where they stand. Their confusion has two major sources. First, I've already noted our culture's traditional prejudice against gays and gayness. Men sometimes don't want to know they're gay. They fear being hated for their identity. Who can blame them? Second, severe abuse or neglect in childhood can lead to sexual compulsions that confuse the truth of a man's identity. Generally, the man must undergo a course of therapy to remove the layers of confusion caused by the childhood abuse.

1. *The beach test.* Gay men notice the men on a beach and don't notice the women. "That man is hot!" a gay man might say. In my experience, straight men, even those who have sex with men, don't react this way.

2. *Youthful noticing.* This is the children's version of the beach test. Before puberty, gay boys notice with a kind of giggling delight other boys, just as straight boys do girls. This is a perfectly natural expression of prepubescent identity that straight boys in our society typically get to share out loud with their peers and gay boys typically do not. Gay men often report to me memories of youthful noticing of boys; straight men

never do. Gay men will often say they didn't know what it meant at the time, but they recall being strongly drawn to another boy their age or preoccupied with another male on television. Only looking back can these gay men understand that their interest was romantic and sexual.

3. *Waking up.* Who do you want to wake up next to, a man or a woman? Some straight guys will kiss and hug other men and so forth, but they still don't want to wake up next to a man. Something is just "off-putting" to a straight guy about the morning light on a face full of stubble.

4. *Falling in love.* No matter how much quick or anonymous sex a gay man might have engaged in, he loves everything about other men: their faces, their chest hair, their deep voices, their humor, their penises. A straight man who has sex with other men (or has fantasies about it or watches gay porn) is most often compulsively focused on certain male body parts or on certain sex acts or sexual scenarios. A gay man yearns for an entire man, not just parts of a man. Gay men can—and often do—fall in romantic love with other men; straight men never do.

5. *Romantic hopes and dreams with a male partner.* After a period of promiscuous "gay adolescence," which will occur typically for a few years after a gay man comes out, he will tend to mature beyond a frantic need to express his newfound sexual freedom and yearn to "settle down" with a loving male partner.

> *Gay Adolescence*—A period of a few years' sexual promiscuity by a gay man that follows his coming out.

6. *Gay sex not degrading.* Out gay men don't feel degraded by their sexuality. Straight men sometimes interpret gay sex as humiliating. For some religious moralists, the core of their objection to homosexuality is a repugnance for dehumanizing acts. However, gay men find gay sex fundamentally joyful, not degrading.

7. *Homophobia.* Gay men unconscious of their gayness are much more homophobic than are straight men who have sex with men. Straight men who are confused and questioning come into my office and say, "I don't think I'm gay, but I might be. If I'm gay, help me just go ahead and come out and be gay." These men are tortured by the thought that they might be fighting the coming-out process.

If a gay man is repressing his gay identity, he is often extremely negative about gay people and the "gay lifestyle." He might complain that gay life is oversexualized, gays are too effeminate, and gay men never have successful relationships. In therapy, these homophobic gay men hope the therapist will make them straight, not help them come out as gay.

* * *

This chapter has considered the marriage between Tom and Jennifer mainly from Jennifer's point of view. She's discovered that Tom has been having sex with a man. She's devastated, hurt, and angry. She's afraid he'll discover that he's gay and leave her. He says he's straight. What's going on? We've considered some of the main issues: What does it mean to be gay? Why might a straight man be interested in sex with men? In chapter 2, Tom tells his side of the story. He insists that he's not gay and that he loves Jennifer and wants to make a family with her. We consider what is motivating Tom's behavior in more detail and what the possible options will be for Tom and Jennifer.

2

TOM'S COMPULSION

Why Would a Straight Man Want To Have Sex with Men?

Self-compassion often increases when a patient comes to see how a disturbing behavior or feeling was formed in childhood.

—Michael Bader[1]

If you had asked Tom what he was looking for on Craigslist, he would have made up something. "I just want to see if anyone could use our old computer." He would have lied without thinking about it, but he wouldn't have been able to tell the truth, even if he had wanted to. He didn't know what he was looking for.

Whatever was guiding him took him to the Men-Seeking-Men personal ads: "Any str8 men bi-curious?" and "Off today. Looking to get fucked. You host." The pictures with some of these went straight to the point: erect penises, without legs, arms, torsos, or faces. "Like what you see? E-mail me."

Tom *was* curious. Were there other married straight guys out there who were curious, too? Should he look for someone gay? It wasn't an overwhelming urge at first, but looking excited him. Lots of the ads said they were from straight men: "My wife will be out of town. I'd like to give it a try. I'm curious." Tom felt relief as well as excitement. *There are other men like me: married, straight, curious.* Soon he was looking more and more, whenever he was sure Jennifer wouldn't walk in on him.

Why am I doing this? he wondered. *I'm not gay.* But he couldn't deny that those pictures grabbed him, those pictures with just a penis, not the bare chests or the full figures. He loved those penis pictures. He wanted to suck a penis. He didn't know why. He didn't know what was exciting him, but the excitement kept drawing him back. *Could I be gay?* he wondered. *If some guy told me he was acting like this, I'd figure he was gay.*

He started responding to the ads. "Hey, I'm straight, too. I just want to jerk off with a man. Try it out. See what it's like." Sometimes, they'd talk on the phone. "You're married? I'm married, too. Want to meet up?" They'd arrange a meeting, then he wouldn't have the courage to go. Then he'd go, and the other guy wouldn't show. He realized a lot of Craigslist contacts must end in "no-shows." Even the ads would say, "Real tired of fakes." And he knew sometimes he was one of those fakes. The fantasy was hot; the reality was scary.

Brad was the first to show. It was as simple as that. They'd e-mailed a dozen times. Talked some on the phone. Finally, they met at a Starbucks. They mostly talked about computers and politics, parted after twenty minutes without talking about sex or making any plans. When Brad e-mailed the following week, inviting Tom over to his house for a beer and maybe some porn, Tom decided to risk it. He told Jennifer he was working late.

He was very excited on the way over. He felt no fear. He was too aroused to be afraid. He was trembling as he knocked on Brad's door. His heart was beating as if he'd run all the way instead of driving.

"Hi, Tom," Brad had said. "Want that beer?"

They sat in Brad's kitchen drinking beer, not talking much, looking over Brad's porn DVDs to make a choice.

Before they went in the living room, Brad said, "This is between us. Agreed? We won't talk about it to anyone, no Facebook posts, no nothing."

Tom nodded. "Sure. We're in the same boat. You could ruin my life. I could ruin yours."

The living room had two big comfortable chairs in front of the TV with a couch in between. "You can sit there," Brad suggested, pointing to one of the chairs. "I'll sit here," he said, taking the other. Brad started the straight-porn DVD they'd chosen. Tom loosened and lowered his pants. Brad was over in his chair doing his thing, having nothing to do with

Tom. After fifteen minutes, Tom cleaned himself up and met Brad back in the kitchen. They had another beer.

"Gotta get home," Tom said after his beer was half gone. He stood. "Hey, it was great."

"Yeah," Brad agreed. "I had a good time." And that was all there was to it.

In a month, they e-mailed again. Soon after, Tom was back in Brad's house. Over time, their activities became more interactive. The first time Tom sucked Brad off, Brad wanted to hold him afterward, even kiss, but Tom wasn't interested.

"We're just trying stuff," Brad coaxed. "Why not try, you know, different stuff?"

"That's okay," Tom said, not wanting Brad to feel bad about it. "I just don't want to."

When they moved on to anal sex, it was because Tom suggested it. Brad was surprised that Tom was so sure he wanted to receive and not give, but he insisted on it. Brad was cheerful when they were done, wanted to cuddle, wanted to go out to Subway for some sandwiches, but Tom felt dirty and dissatisfied. He left immediately after. Yet, he kept coming back.

Often, driving home after being with Brad, Tom found himself wishing they could just meet without the sex. That didn't make any sense. They were meeting *because* of the sex. Tom was always excited before seeing Brad, but the sex wasn't exciting, and when it was over he usually felt he hadn't gotten what he wanted. Still, he liked meeting with Brad.

He and Brad met fifteen times over two years. They took care to avoid their two wives, but that wasn't difficult. Brad's wife traveled a lot on business, and Jennifer accepted that Tom often had to work late. Still, Tom had close calls. Once Jennifer came up behind Tom after he thought she was asleep, and he barely had time to change the tab to keep her from seeing an e-mail from Brad.

Another time, he came home with his pants unzipped. Jennifer teased him about what people must have been thinking at work. He laughed with her, but he was terrified that she'd guess something was going on.

Even though he took pains to keep his secret from her, Tom didn't feel he was cheating on Jennifer. He was happy with his wife, his marriage, and their sexual relationship. This thing with Brad was about something else. Tom just didn't know what. He supposed he might be gay, but he didn't feel gay.

Tom was excited and anxiety-free only in those brief moments when he was on his way to see Brad and before they had sex. At all other times, he couldn't stop worrying about being found out by Jennifer, and he worried that he might be gay. The sex with Brad was okay, but afterward Tom was always dissatisfied. "Maybe that means I'm not really gay," he told himself, "but if I'm not gay, why did I get into this in the first place?"

WHAT'S REALLY GOING ON FOR TOM?

Tom came into my office and sat in the chair by the door. I asked him how he was doing, and he gave me a sad shake of his head.

"If only I'd deleted those e-mails," he told me. "Then I wouldn't be in all this trouble."

"I'm surprised," I said, "that you asked Jennifer to look for something on *that* computer."

"I thought I'd hidden everything." Tom shrugged. "I forgot about it. I don't know. Anyway, I'm ready to talk. I haven't had anybody to talk to."

He filled me in on the whole two years with Brad.

"It must have been very lonely for you," I said.

"I don't think I'm gay," he told me, " but can you help me with that?"

I took him through my basic evaluation: The beach test, youthful noticing, defensive homophobia, and so forth as listed at the end of chapter 1. I asked him, "Did you ever want to spoon with Brad? Did you feel like you were falling for him?"

"No," Tom said. "Not at all."

I told him that sometimes gay or bi men who don't know they are gay or bi start out just as he did. They begin seeing men out of erotic curiosity, and often they are unhappy after their first few sexual encounters, because as they begin to feel a growing realization that they are gay or bi, it can be very upsetting. However, when they have more sexual experiences with men, they begin to feel more connected to the men *and* to the sex. Straight men may enjoy the sex but don't tend to become emotionally attached to the men they are hooking up with.

"Now that you mention it," Tom said, "Brad wanted to hug and kiss, and that made me uncomfortable. Ironic, I guess, considering what else we were doing."

Tom had given me the physical details of their sex, but that didn't change my initial impressions. Nothing about Tom was gay. Something else was motivating his behavior.

I always ask a new client about his or her childhood, and I always ask about sexual abuse. Abuse is sometimes subtle and is often forgotten. Tom had been a little vague about his history, so I brought him to focus on various aspects of his relationships with adults when he was a boy.

It's amazing what a man with extreme childhood experiences like Tom can "forget," although memories are not really forgotten. People keep the memory of events but lose a sense of how they felt. As I work to coax a client's story from him, I often hear the phrase, "Well, I don't know if this means anything but . . . ," followed by a horrendous tale of major significance. And so Tom's story unfolded in my office over fifteen sessions, but I'll compress and organize it here for clarity.

Tom didn't have a good father. The man would ridicule him and spank him for no apparent reason. When Tom was five, his father left, and his mother remarried a man with two sons of his own. He favored his own boys and ignored Tom, who grew starved for male approval.

Tom's best friend was Jimmy. Jimmy's dad took an interest in Tom when he learned that Tom's father was gone and his stepdad didn't like him. Jimmy's dad was involved with a kids sports program, an after-school baseball league. All the kids called him "Coach."

"I'll help you with sports," he told Tom. "I'll take you under my wing." It seemed so wonderful. His best friend's dad liked him. Coach praised him constantly. "You've got good hands. The ball never gets away from you. You're my favorite guy on the team."

This special attention was noticeable. Jimmy even seemed a little jealous. "God, my dad really likes you."

The sex began when Tom was ten, a sleepover at Jimmy's house. It was late. They were watching TV, but Jimmy had fallen asleep. Coach took out his erect penis and let Tom see it. "You need somebody to teach you about your body," Coach said. "How it works. Not a big deal. Skin is skin. Take yours out, and I'll show you." And so Jimmy's father taught Tom how to masturbate. They masturbated together every so often for several months, and then Coach showed Tom how they could masturbate each other.

Over the next few years, Coach subverted Tom's intuitive understanding that his body was private and no one had a right to touch it. Coach knew many ways to get past Tom's defenses. Sexual predators understand this "grooming" process very well.

"He used to crack me on the ass with his towel when I got out of the shower," Tom told me, "but that was just his way of making a joke. Later he'd smack me with his hand. Then he'd rub my butt to take away the sting."

"You'd be naked?"

"Yes."

"Coach used to want to dry me off when I got out of the shower. I felt funny about it, but it showed me how special I was for him. He really liked me."

"Do you realize now," I asked him, "that that's really highly unusual?"

"I haven't thought about it," Tom replied. "He liked me. I was his most valuable player."

Coach would come out of the shower naked, act like it was nothing between men, but then play with Tom, touch him, smack his butt, rub his butt, handle his penis.

"No big deal," Coach told him. "You don't have a father to help you learn about sex. You need me to educate you."

Coach told Tom he would need to know how to do it one day with girls, but meanwhile he taught Tom to have anal sex with him. He began by fingering Tom's buttocks, saying things like, "Fucking an ass is just like fucking a pussy. A hole's a hole."

By the time Tom was in the seventh grade he was regularly receiving anal sex from Coach. The logic that he should be giving and not receiving to prepare for his heterosexual future didn't occur to him. But really, for Tom this was about pleasing Coach, not pleasing himself. Tom would have done anything for "Dad."

Still, when Tom was in the eighth grade, he decided he really didn't like this stuff with Coach. He got up the courage to say, "I don't want to do this anymore. It doesn't feel right to me. I think I really like girls."

The coach's response was quick and brutal. "You're off the team. I don't want to have anything to do with you. We're done. It's over." And, just as suddenly, Jimmy wouldn't have anything to do with Tom either. Tom had lost his father figure and his best friend in a single blow.

He was more than devastated, but afterward something strange happened. He forgot about it.

CHILDHOOD ABUSE AND HOMOSEXUAL-BEHAVIORAL IMPRINTING

A man can suffer sexual abuse as a boy, forget it after he grows up, and then "mysteriously" find that he is drawn to sex with men even though he isn't gay. This was Tom's story. Childhood sexual abuse is the number-one reason a straight man will have a compulsion to seek sex with men. (Straight men will seek sex with men for a variety of other reasons. See chapter 16.)

Compulsive behavior differs from sexual attraction. A man controlled by a compulsion is driven by the abuse. Tom was reenacting what happened to him with his coach. I've treated many men like Tom, and their stories all follow the same pattern: First, some significant childhood sexual abuse happens; it could be a single event, such as a rape, or it could unfold over years, as in Tom's case. Second, the abuse penetrates the boy's psyche through shame and stays there because it is given no outlet. It is "forgotten."

As an adult, he returns to the scene of the sexual crime. He may arrange sexual encounters with men, as Tom did with Brad, or be obsessed with fantasies of doing so. On the other hand, he may have an opposite compulsion and be caught in the grip of an obsessive homophobia. How can you tell that adult sex-drenched thoughts and behaviors are being driven by an underlying childhood trauma? Because they feel separate from the rest of the man. They are, in psychological terms, "unintegrated." To the individual, they can feel like demonic possession: "someone else" takes over for a time, and when the spell is over, the person is left confused and "abandoned," wondering what happened and feeling very uneasy about it. Unhappy endings are typical. Trauma-driven sex almost never leads to relationships.

Trauma—The psychological difficulties that can result from abuse. The trauma is the result of the abuse, the "damage." Typically, it manifests in compulsive behaviors, addictions, and many other states of unhappiness such as chronic depression and anxiety disorders.

The reason the sex can't be connected to the rest of the man's life is that the "acting entity" isn't the adult man but rather the ghost of a frightened child trying to tell its story. Therapy helps by giving this child his own voice and allowing it to be heard and put to rest. I purposefully use the language of the supernatural, because it is the closest metaphor in common usage. I could restate what I'm saying in standard psychological terminology, but that language can come off as mere psychobabble. Yet this "ghost sex" is real. I see it all the time in my office.

Maybe I should note here that Tom's abuse need not have been so overt for it to have troubled him as an adult. We've already talked about the "grooming" of a victim by a perpetrator. Grooming begins with subtle forms of sexual suggestion and touch that precede the more overt sexual activity that involves genital contact. But the grooming alone can cause trauma to a child. The coach showered with Tom, dried him off after, and slapped his butt. This was covert abuse. Another example (which Tom didn't report) is sleeping naked in the same bed without there being any touching. A typical behavior would be commenting on the boy's genitals—"One day you'll have one like me," or "You'll get to be like this some day"; or complimenting the boy's equipment—"You're hung like a man now."

What my clients report are incidents where the adult's intent is sexual, but the adult is pretending nothing is happening, never acting "sexual" in an overt way. The kid wouldn't have words for it, but he would know. He would pick up the vibes. They would leave him feeling dirty, and he would typically think that he'd done something dirty. He'd think, "What did I do to make that happen?" He'd feel "icky."

It's subtle and yet not. The residue into adulthood is definite: his psyche's saying, "Something's here. You better deal with it and heal it."

Some people will say: Oh, come on. Plenty of boys are sexually abused or hazed or bullied, and they don't grow up to have sex fantasies about men. That's true, but the trauma may manifest itself in other ways.

Some of my abused clients are violently homophobic. They've confused the abuse with homosexuality. Others have developed damaging addictions to sex, drugs, food, or other substances or behaviors.

TOM AND BRAD GO THEIR SEPARATE WAYS

When Tom and Brad first met, they were both confused. Both were married; neither thought he was gay, but each thought he might be. Each felt compelled to meet a guy for sex.

Tom was drawn to the sex with Brad, but when it was over he didn't feel he'd gotten anywhere. He was still confused. He felt dissatisfied. Yet, he kept coming back to Brad.

As time went on, Brad told Tom he wanted to get to know him better. He suggested they have dinner. He offered for Tom to spend the night. Tom didn't want any of that.

Tom called Brad a "buddy," but the truth was they weren't anything like friends. When Tom got together with Brad, it was like Tom was in a trance. He had been abused between the ages of nine and fourteen; when he was with Brad, he felt that young. He wasn't *there* as a man to be with Brad. For Tom, Brad was a character in a story from his childhood. And the situation Tom found himself in was very confusing. He didn't really want to be having sex with Brad, but he felt compelled to do it. Something drew him to the sex, something that promised to feel right and good but that always evaporated with his orgasm.

Finally, Brad said one night, "Hey, let's go away for a weekend," and Tom was so shocked, he momentarily came out of his trance. Soon after, he told Brad he couldn't see him anymore.

Then, Jennifer found the e-mails, and Tom came to see me. I told him that Brad was most likely gay and coming out. The different reactions of Brad and Tom to each other illustrate the difference between a confused gay man coming out and a straight man acting out his childhood trauma. Brad was falling for Tom and wanted to spend more time with him and become romantic. Tom was not falling for Brad and didn't have romantic feelings toward him at all.

THE UNCONSCIOUS MIND: YOUR SILENT PARTNER

When Tom finds Brad and starts meeting with him for sex, Tom is not seeking a sex partner, or expressing his sexuality, or seeking a friend. He is hypnotically enacting a script from his childhood, like the brainwashed assassin in the movie *The Manchurian Candidate*. Like that assassin, he is carrying out the orders of another person, his younger self embedded in his unconscious mind. Tom must repeatedly enact his abuse until he hears and understands the message of grief that it encodes. One of the main functions of therapy is to open up a healthy channel for these messages.

> *Unconscious Mind*—Also called "the unconscious." A part of the mind that operates outside of normal awareness but can create powerful processes that influence daily life. The logic of the unconscious mind is not "ordinary" logic, and the mechanisms that the unconscious creates to deal with past psychological trauma may cause unrelenting grief in the present until a therapeutic intervention is effective.

WHAT IN YOUR MAN'S PAST SHOULD GIVE YOU PAUSE?

Either overt or covert childhood sexual abuse can leave a residue of trauma. Tom's abuse started out covert, via Coach's extended program of "grooming," but then the abuse went overt, meaning it involved the genitals.

Covert sexual abuse is a sexual encounter that does not involve physical sexual contact. A client once told me that his mother had him take down his pants because "You're sixteen. I want to see if your penis is developing." In another case, an aunt refused to cover her breasts in the presence of her sister's teenage son. "These little things," she'd say. "They're not worth noticing." But the boy *was* bothered by his topless aunt. These last two cases are examples of covert sexual abuse, which can have significant and long-lasting traumatic effects on a child. [2]

Coach's behavior in the locker room, the touching and the slapping and the sexual talk, all constituted covert sexual abuse of Tom. Had

Coach been prevented from raping Tom, he probably would still have suffered from this covert abuse.

I use the following types of questions in therapy, when the therapeutic process has reached a point that I can do so productively. I don't expect a person to have much opportunity to use them with a partner outside of a therapeutic setting, but they do illustrate further what constitutes overt and covert abuse.

In childhood or young adolescence,
Overt:

1. Did anyone masturbate your penis?
2. Did anyone ever put their mouth on your penis?
3. Did you ever put your mouth or hands on a man's genitals?

Covert:

1. Did anyone ever comment on your developing body in ways that made you uncomfortable or feel icky?
2. Did anyone ever look longer than they should at your crotch or genitals?
3. Did anyone ever make inappropriate comments about how you express your masculinity?
4. Were you able to lock the bathroom door?
5. Did anyone tell you that you had to leave the shower open while they were in the bathroom?
6. Did you ever sleep with a parent or adult where they or both of you were naked?

TOM'S THERAPY

Over a course of treatment lasting several years, Tom stopped feeling the need to act out his abuse. He still had occasional fantasies, but his need to act on them had left him. The therapy involved weekly individual and group therapy. Tom read some books on males who have been sexually abused (see below), and he made use of resources such as MaleSurvivor: National Organization against Male Sexual Victimization[3] and Oprah's Sexual Abuse Resource Center.[4] I helped him find and express his grief and anger over what his coach, his friend's father, had done to him. Aside from the disgust and repulsion he felt at being abused, he was particularly devastated that he had been so betrayed by a trusted father figure.

Also, let's note here that sexual abuse cannot change someone's orientation, which is set at birth. What sexual abuse can do is cloud a man's ability to know himself. It can cause him to act out in the same ways he was abused. This homosexual-behavioral imprinting is not about orientation or identity; it's about trauma and abuse influencing behavior.

Men dealing with child sex abuse at one time had few resources for healing, and they often had to endure an attitude of skepticism and ridicule, even from helping professionals. However, now that the prevalence of this abuse and the harm it does is more generally acknowledged, a number of organizations offer help. A good place to start is www.malesurvivor.org. Also, excellent books that provide information and affirmation include *Abused Boys: The Neglected Victims of Sexual Abuse*,[5] *Victims No Longer: The Classic Guide for Men Recovering from Sexual Child Abuse*,[6] and *Betrayed as Boys: Psychodynamic Treatment of Sexually Abused Men*.[7]

JENNIFER DEALS WITH HER REACTIONS

Understandably, Jennifer felt deeply the betrayal of a woman with an unfaithful spouse. She had trusted Tom so completely; she was caught so off guard. For a while, listening to her anger and her anguish was all we did in therapy. She told Tom and she told me just how devastated she felt, and I cautioned Tom to listen and not interrupt. She needed him to hear her, especially as she dealt with the first shock of his betrayal. I gave her a copy of Stephanie Carnes's *Mending a Shattered Heart*,[8] which contains my chapter on women involved with men who have had sex with men. Recovering her trust with Tom was a matter of years of incremental improvement. These years included therapy for Tom, of course, and for the two of them, and eventually for her also.

Her anger at Tom wasn't decreasing, despite her understanding that his behavior was the result of being sexually abused as a child. I felt that her own issues must be fueling her rage, and I suggested individual therapy for her, either with me or another therapist. In therapy, she remembered that her father had had an affair that grieved her mother deeply and put a pall of gloom over her childhood. Jennifer carried the grief of these childhood memories into her marriage. It was activated when she learned of Tom's infidelity. Her therapy included expressing the pain she had silently absorbed at home as a child. She needed to heal not only from the trauma of Tom's behavior, but also from this older wound.

TOM AND JENNIFER WORKING TOGETHER

Throughout his long therapeutic journey, Tom came to understand that he not only had to work hard on his own childhood issues, but he had to work to repair the rupture he had created in his marriage.

The hardest part for him was having to listen to Jennifer express her anger, sadness, and pain about what he had done. At first, he thought they could have one or two conversations, and it would be over. That is not how it goes. I taught him to listen to her, to be patient and validate what she told him. Not that Jennifer was allowed to choose any time and any length of time to punish Tom with her words, her feelings, and her betrayal. I taught them both to make appointments and set time limits, so that they would talk about it only when both were ready and willing to do so. The rule was that they were to find a time within twenty-four hours of the request.

Most people who cheat and feel bad about it don't want to listen to their partner's pain, because they caused it. This was the case with Tom. I worked with him to understand the importance of listening to Jennifer over an indefinite period of time so she could work through her trauma around his cheating.

Tom and Jennifer did manage to save their marriage. Tom's therapy relieved him of his need to act out. Jennifer was willing give Tom a chance to earn back her trust. When last I heard, they were still together.

I've laid out this much detail on the story of Tom and Jennifer to give a sense of what can be involved in recovery when sexual secrets are allowed to build up and poison a marriage. It can take five years to restore trust even with goodwill and good therapeutic support.

* * *

Often, when a woman comes to me to seek advice about her "gay husband," it turns out he isn't gay. Many "signs of gayness" are signs of
other problems. Sometimes "kinky sex" is really gayness, and sometimes
it's just kinky sex, as we see with Joel and Sherri in the next chapter.

3

AN IRRESISTIBLE HUMILIATION
Joel Loves Cuckolding

It may seem eccentric that my husband has translated the common fear of being cheated on into enthusiasm for the idea, but he's not alone.

—Ada Calhoun [1]

They met for coffee at a nearby Starbucks, because as soon as they began the scene, they would all be expected to remain "in character." Joel thought the woman was maybe a little older than his thirty-five. The man was even older, but Joel didn't care about him. She acknowledged that often in these scenes the real husband would be the submissive, but in this case they wanted Joel to play the submissive husband and the real husband to play the extra, "superior," man. That's what they'd discussed in their e-mails, but she wanted to make sure Joel understood the rules. In a way, his part was going to be easy. He just had to do what she told him to do from the moment he entered their house until he left.

"Oh, yes," she reminded him. "No sex for you, but you *will* be mostly naked."

He was so excited he could hardly drive the few blocks to their house. The woman greeted him at the door with a cold, disapproving sneer. She had put up her hair in a bun and had changed into a long grey dress and heels. She immediately ordered him to strip and then acted impatient as he fumbled off his clothes. He had worried he might have a very out-of-character erection, but that was hardly a problem at the moment. When he stood before her naked, her sneer became even more pronounced. "You are a disappointing shit, aren't you?" she said.

Then she ordered him to put on a wig, pantyhose, and lipstick. She made him stand in front of the hall mirror. "You look like the bitch you were meant to be!" she told him, turned, and started walking away, so he followed.

In the bedroom, the man was dressed in black, including a black leather jacket. Joel was ordered to his knees, and the couple talked about what a ridiculous miserable excuse for a husband he was. "I'm so lucky," she told the man, "you came along, so I wouldn't have to endure the humiliation of this little shit's pitiful lovemaking anymore. Look at his tiny dick. What a joke!"

She ordered Joel to undo the man's pants and get him hard. Joel's heart was beating a million miles an hour. On his knees, he rolled a condom onto the man's already stiffening member. He rubbed the cock and gave it a few sucks. The woman held Joel's hair in a firm, almost painful grasp and moved his head up and down. It didn't take long before she was satisfied. She pushed Joel away and turned so she could be entered from behind. Joel was allowed only to watch, which was fine with him. He was a little shit and could expect nothing better.

When they finished, she ordered Joel to discard the condom and clean up both of them with a damp towel. Then he was dismissed. He dressed alone in the front hall and left.

Joel returned home after Sherri had already gone to bed. He stayed downstairs and paced, but he couldn't quell his excitement. He went into the bathroom and masturbated. That gave him only momentary relief. He was excited. He was worried. He knew he was not gay. Absolutely no way. He was not even bisexual. But that night he had performed oral sex on a man. This was no fantasy. It was for real. What if Sherri found out? He wasn't being unfaithful. He wasn't having sex with anybody, not exactly, but she would never understand.

A horrified thought occurred to him. There had been a condom, but maybe something had spilled out. Had he gotten any of the man's semen on his clothes? He didn't think so, but he stripped and hid everything he'd been wearing in a garbage bag, even his shoes. He showered and scrubbed himself raw. He brushed his teeth twice. Was that enough? Had he really put that stranger's penis in his mouth? Condoms failed sometimes. They sometimes had tiny holes in them. Joel had read about that.

He went and pulled the Clorox from under the kitchen sink. Maybe he should gargle with this? God. How could he suck some guy's cock? And some guy he didn't even know.

Joel had to admit it was hot. He had been excited. Just thinking about it made him excited again. He absently started stroking himself right there in the kitchen. He loved the way the woman had ordered him to do it. She was the strict woman of his dreams. He would have done almost anything for her. Had he been unfaithful? No. He hadn't had sex with anyone, had he? Could he catch a disease? Could he give Sherri a disease? Could he get HIV or some STD just from oral sex in a condom? Maybe. And how would he know if he had gotten something? What if he got something and then gave it to Sherri? He didn't think so, but you never could tell.

He poured an inch of Clorox into a glass. Maybe he should add some water. He looked on the bottle for a clue to how much. *Directions. Warning. Poison Control Center number.* Poison? Damn, this stuff was poison! What was he doing?

He couldn't go upstairs to their bedroom. He didn't want to get close to Sherri. He felt too guilty and ashamed. He fell asleep on the couch in the family room at 3 a.m., exhausted with fear and excitement.

Cuckolding—Sexual fantasy in which a husband watches his wife have sex with a "superior" man.

The next day Joel decided he had gone too far. He swore to himself he'd never meet with a couple again. He could make do with porn. He usually allowed himself his "porn hour," 10 to 11 p.m., while Sherri was watching her TV shows. Tonight, he found his favorite cuckolding site and masturbated to it. As he went down at 11 to watch TV with Sherri, he thought, "Maybe porn could be enough. Why take risks getting hooked up with couples?" He sat by Sherri and held her hand. She smiled and snuggled up next to him as *The Daily Show* started.

Joel had tried to talk to Sherri about his fantasies: The one where he was the "humiliated helper" for a husband and wife, or even better the one where his wife, Sherri, would do it with another man while he helped them. He didn't get a good response from her on that. He wanted Sherri at least to watch porn with him, but when he kind of suggested it she kind of said no. He was too ashamed to come right out and ask. He didn't want to deal with her mocking his fantasy. It was too important to him.

Porn—The definition of pornography is surprisingly elusive, both legally and socially. In this book, when we refer to porn, we mean movies (or pictures or books or other works) created to arouse viewers sexually. Legally, a work tends not to be classified as "porn" unless it involves sex acts (genitals in action). On the other hand, some of my clients are turned on by faces being slapped or a pretty amputee walking on crutches. Porn can also include dramatic situations, such as a cuckolding scene, which might show no overt sexual activity.

After ten years of marriage, they'd drifted into once-a-week sex, usually Saturday morning. Pleasant enough, but Joel was vaguely aware that he might want more if he wasn't watching so much porn and she wasn't watching so much television. He had no idea what Sherri wanted. She didn't initiate sex, and they never talked about it.

Sherri came home from work most nights late and tired. Joel had his own construction company. Many nights he worked later than Sherri, but other days he wasn't that busy. They had supper together when they could, but often they were just not in sync. If he felt like it, Joel had a lot of opportunities to get lost in porn, or more.

He'd found the couple to "play with" on a cuckolding website where lots of couples and individuals ran ads looking for play partners. He'd contacted half a dozen people through ads and message boards and websites. Mostly, they were men who would tell him they were looking for other men to do their wives. He also spoke to men looking for couples. Joel pretended his wife was interested, just to see if it might lead to something.

Over the week after he met with them, he couldn't get the couple out of his mind, the black-leather dude and the "Mistress." Against his better judgment, because he could imagine the many risks he was taking, he arranged to meet with them again. This time, when he showed up, it was the man who opened the door. Dressed in black as before, he greeted Joel with a silent smirk and led him back to the bedroom. The man indicated that Joel was to strip and get on his knees, but the woman wasn't there. Although the rules of the play were that Joel couldn't speak, this wasn't what he'd signed up for.

"Where's Mistress?" he asked.

The man had the grace to look a little embarrassed. "She couldn't make it," he admitted. "Her mother got sick, and she had to go out of town. But we can still do things."

"She's not here?" Joel said, a note of panic entering his voice.

"I just figured we could do some things like we did before. Then next time she'll be here."

"No way," Joel said. "If she's not here, I'm not interested." He backed to the door as if a tiger were in the room.

"Don't freak," the man said. "Okay. I guess I should have told you. Why don't we just have a drink, talk? What do you drink? I've got most stuff."

"No way," Joel repeated. "I'm leaving." When he saw the grieved look on the man's face, he paused. "Look. I'm not angry or anything. It just doesn't work for me without her."

"Sure," the man said. "Next time she'll be here. "

Joel was truly turned off by the idea of being with the man alone. *She* had to be there, or the fantasy was ruined. Joel was more disgusted with himself than by the man. It was his own fault. He was taking too many risks. He'd made the decision to stick with porn, and here he was trying to set up a scene again. From now on, he really would stick with porn. Porn was safe.

He didn't think he was being unfaithful with Sherri. Not technically. But what kind of marriage had they drifted into over the past ten years? He couldn't talk about it with her. He wanted to, but he couldn't. He had too much to tell. The habit of not talking was too ingrained. He felt too ashamed.

Then one day he came home from work early and found himself dialing the couple's number, trembling with excitement, lost in his fantasy, until the man answered and Joel hung up. He was horrified. What had he been doing? He decided if he couldn't talk with Sherri, he'd have to find someone else to talk with. He'd already gotten my number. He called me right then for an appointment.

THE HOT WIFE

The afternoon I met Joel, he was wearing a tie with a short-sleeved shirt. His hair was cut short, and he looked younger than his actual mid-thirties.

He apologized for the sweat stains under his arms but explained he'd spent the morning at a worksite. His company was restoring some old office buildings, and he believed "the boss" should be seen "getting his hands dirty" as much as possible. He told me he'd learned general construction from his father, and business was booming as the recession eased. A few years before, he'd had to lay off four men, but now he'd been able to rehire them all. Work, of course, wasn't what he'd come to talk about with me.

He told me he was watching porn, and he'd met a couple once, and he was beginning to feel out of control with it, because he'd tried to stop but couldn't. It was taking up too much of his life, and maybe it was getting in the way of his marriage.

"I want to tell Sherri," he said. "I hate doing these things behind her back, but if I tell her, she'd probably think I'm gay or crazy or both. She'd probably want a divorce, but I'm not really doing anything wrong. Not really."

"Why don't you tell me from the beginning?" I suggested.

It started (he told me) when his young wife, Sherri, went to California for a summer internship. They were both undergraduates at Michigan State. She was majoring in public relations; he, in business. The internship was a wonderful opportunity for her, a chance to get experience at a major consulting firm, but it would take her away from Michigan for almost four whole months. Joel wasn't happy about that.

Joel and Sherri had been high school sweethearts. They decided not to marry until they finished college, and then they couldn't wait and married anyway after their sophomore year. Her absence for the internship was between their junior and senior years. It was difficult for both of them, because they were already used to married life together, but Joel had an especially unexpected reaction to his wife's absence.

The moment she left he was afraid she would get involved with somebody, and as soon as he discovered that her closest intern coworker was a guy named Karl, he was sure of it.

He spent the summer obsessing about how long she took to answer his e-mails and phone messages. He felt suspicious of Sherri as he never had before. She explained to him how busy she was with the internship, which made sense, but after she told him about Karl, he was frantic with jealousy. He'd never experienced anything like this before.

"Aren't you a little bit too close to this Karl character?" he asked her. "I bet he's the type who's always hitting on you."

Her response was a shocked, "Don't be ridiculous. We're both working hard to make a good impression, and we help each other. That's all there is to it."

Joel *knew* differently. He stole her passwords and after that regularly monitored all her e-mails, especially with Karl. They did e-mail each other, but Joel found nothing sexual or romantic.

He made it kind of a joke. "Are you fucking Karl yet?" he would e-mail her.

"Are you still being ridiculous?" she would reply.

Then, to his horror, he found himself masturbating to a fantasy of Sherri and Karl going at it. He imagined himself a watcher, not a participant. That was an important detail in the fantasy. She *made* him watch, *wouldn't let* him participate. He was confused and bothered by his fantasy, because in reality the idea of Sherri being unfaithful was very painful to him, but in the fantasy it was a major turn-on.

She came back from her internship and never communicated with Karl again, but by then Joel's fantasy was firmly embedded in his sexual imagination. He loved Sherri and believed she had been faithful, but this fantasy began to take over a bigger and bigger part of his life.

Somewhat to his surprise, Joel discovered online that the fantasy of a man watching his wife have sex with another man was a common porn theme. The woman controls the scene. She "forces" her husband to endure the humiliation of seeing her have sex with a "superior" man; and in some versions of the fantasy, the husband has to "help" in some submissive way, say by cleaning up after, or even by having sex with the man at the woman's command. This fantasy has been given the label "cuckolding," from the word "cuckold," whose traditional meaning is a man whose wife is adulterous. Another term is also used: "hotwifing," a mashup of "hot" and "wife." The "hot wife" is too "hot" to stay faithful to her husband.

On the Internet, thousands of porn sites cater to men turned on by cuckolding. Website names go from the subtle "I Play and He Waits," to the overt "My Pathetic Cuckold Hubby" and "Humiliated Hubbies," to the crude "Fuck My Wife" and "I Will Fuck Your Wife." Once Joel discovered these porn sites, he couldn't stay away from them.

After graduation, while he and Sherri were starting their "normal" married life together, while his construction company blossomed and her internship had led to a good position with an established company, Joel's secret life became more and more important to him. He masturbated to cuckolding porn sites, and this form of sexual release became indispensable to him.

Joel would bliss out imagining his hot wife and her lover. He would lose himself in sexual daydreams at his desk when he had deadlines pressing. He'd go online for porn at home while Sherri was busy working late. He had no idea why imagining his "hot" wife "forcing" him to watch her have sex with a "superior" man turned him on so much, but he found it irresistible.

WHAT IT ALL MEANS

Mostly, I didn't interrupt as Joel filled me in. I let him tell his story, but then I had many questions that we discussed over his next few sessions. I asked if he was turned on by porn involving two women and one man, and he told me, "Yes." I asked if he was interested in threeways with two men and one woman, and the men were kissing and mutually giving each other oral sex. He told me, "No." That scene was a *turn-off*, he assured me. He told me he didn't enjoy gay porn either. Joel was never attracted to the men in the fantasy. It mattered how the wife looked, not how the man looked, except Joel wanted him to have a big cock.

"What if the woman were to leave the scene," I asked him, "and it was just you and the husband?" Joel responded like every other guy I've treated with this fantasy. He said he would be turned off. He said that if the husband were to leave, though, that would turn him on.

I quickly went through my usual checklist for gay men, but I already knew Joel wasn't gay. His responses were typical of straight men who are into cuckolding. I told him he wasn't gay or bi.

"Then what's it about?" he asked. "Why does this thing turn me on so much if I'm not gay?"

"Men often get attached to some specific thing and give it special sexual significance," I told him. "There are some technical terms and some technical distinctions, but let me simplify all that. Let's just call it a 'kink.' You have a kink for cuckolding.

"Straight men tend to have a number of kinks that are commonly confused with being gay," I told him. "Interest in cuckolding is one of them. I know you'll find 'experts' in the blogosphere who'll assure you with absolute confidence that an interest in cuckolding always goes with being gay or bi, but they are simply wrong. The opposite is true. Never gay. Sometimes bi."

"Okay. Why?"

"There are theories, but none of them are proven," I said. "Nobody really knows why a person finds something specifically arousing. Many people like pretty feet. Some men find feet so exciting that almost nothing else is sexually interesting. We call that a "foot fetish," a kink for feet. Kinks are common for men and much less common for women. They don't require therapy, unless the "kinkster" is getting into trouble or grief around it. A man who crawls around in the college library stealing women's shoes is getting into trouble with his foot fetish and causing trouble for other people. I treated a man who was doing exactly that, and I helped him, but I still couldn't tell him what caused his kink."

Compulsions, addictions, and unmanageable behaviors—A person can be drawn to a behavior that harms his or her health, financial security, job, or causes harm to others. When the person repeats the behavior despite the negative consequences, wants to stop but cannot, and refuses to take effective responsibility for the behavior, then the behavior is "unmanageable" and usually satisfies the technical psychological definition of a compulsion. In the past, if the compulsive behavior included certain drugs or alcohol, it was also called an addiction. Today, the term "addiction" is used to include many compulsive behaviors, including sex addiction, and some controversy exists about what "qualifies" as an addiction. The distinction is academic but has legal, medical, and social-acceptance implications.

"But, I'm not gay?"

"You're not gay. You've reported some compulsive behavior around porn, but I think that's because you're trying to suppress an important component of your sexual self. This cuckolding fantasy isn't just a 'turn-on' for you; it's an important part of who you are."

"So, what do I do?"

"I want to help you accept that you have this fantasy, that it's important to you. I want to help you remove any unhealthy shame you have around it. When you can embrace it as a healthy fantasy, then you won't be so compulsive with it. I want you to be in control of whether or not you act on it. Eventually, you might want to tell your wife about it."

Joel had always thought he should tell his wife, but he'd hardly done more than give her a few hints. He'd never told her he was masturbating in front of the computer at home. (Most men don't tell their wives such things.) He certainty hadn't told her he'd met with a couple to act out a cuckolding scene.

Of course, he didn't want to tell her any of this. He was worried she would think he was gay. He was very worried she would decide he had been unfaithful, even though he didn't think he had been. He wondered if he could get her interested in his kink, but he was afraid she'd shame him for it instead. Still, he hated keeping secrets from her. It was eating him up inside.

I told him I thought he should tell Sherri, but first it might be helpful if we did a few sessions to look at the details of his fantasy and find out, if we could, where it came from. Maybe we could discover together why he had such a strong and specific sexual interest. Usually there are reasons why a person has a strong favorite sexual fantasy, whether or not it's problematic. (See chapter 11 on core sexual scripts.) Often, the reasons are revealed in the circumstances of a person's childhood. Severe childhood abuse tends to create definite fantasies, but many less severe circumstances of childhood also imprint themselves as sexual scripts; for example, (1) a parent who was chronically ill and therefore often absent or (2) a special-needs sibling who absorbed a great deal of the parents' attention and resources. One of the surprising facts about sexual scripts is that they are usually generated by nonsexual stresses.

Joel confessed to me that he was very much ashamed of his sexual fantasy and wanted to get rid of it. I told him that the story contained in his fantasy, the cuckold script, was not his problem. His way of acting out the script and his secrecy with Sherri might be problems. The fantasy itself was not a problem.

Cuckolding is a very common fantasy. Otherwise, thousands of porn sites wouldn't be devoted to it. On my informational website, www. straightguise.com, the page on cuckolding gets more late-night hits than any other page. I suggested he might want to look at psychologist David

Ley's *Insatiable Wives*,[2] which considers cuckolding from a number of angles. I thought the book might help Joel feel less alone in his fascination with the subject.

His shame around it was the most serious problem for him, because it kept him from looking at his behavior and inhibited him from sharing with Sherri. We talked about his feeling that he was neglecting Sherri in favor of his fantasy. I encouraged him to be curious about where the fantasy came from. I told him that once we understood its origins, we could use that understanding to guide his therapeutic process, and it would help him explain to Sherri what was going on.

The goal of therapy is to help people stop recycling in the present trouble from the past. If you consult with me about a "presenting problem," my approach to help you is guided by the concept that what happened in your childhood and early socialization impact the problems you're having now and how you're handling them. I question you about your problems and how they're affecting your life, and I ask for details about your childhood, looking especially for troubled feelings and situations. I will lead you to rediscover old trouble and express the associated feelings (grief, anger) about it that you may not have been able to express sufficiently as a child. This direct expression of feelings from old wounds can be remarkably effective in curing chronic adult dysfunctional behavior.

WHY WAS THE FANTASY SO COMPELLING?

I asked Joel to describe for me the most exciting part of his cuckolding fantasy. He told me it was his humiliation at not being able to be a part of the couple's sexual experience. He was allowed only to watch. He was turned on by the idea of being told that he cannot please his wife as much as her lover can. This guy has a bigger penis than Joel, and his wife ridicules him for not being as big as her lover.

After Joel had become comfortable with me, I decided to try to get even more detail.

"We should think about why your fantasy got more intense," I suggested, "when you became jealous of Sherri that time she went away for the internship."

"I don't think I had the fantasy before that," Joel told me.

"Okay. Why did the fantasy begin when Sherri went on her internship?"

Joel shook his head. "It just came out of nowhere," he told me.

"I'm sure it seemed like that," I said.

I wasn't surprised that we couldn't make direct progress at first on the issue Joel had come to see me about. Usually, I need to work with a client on the context of his childhood and life before we can solve a specific problem.

I began with his childhood. He had been an only child. Even so, one of his core issues concerned the attention he failed to receive from his parents.

"I never felt I was part of my parents' marriage," he said.

"How do you mean?"

"My mother and I had a good time together. When my father was away, she and I were inseparable. I helped her fix supper after I came home from school. She wanted to hear about my day, and I'd go on and on, and she always seemed interested. We went to movies together, and she read to me every night before tucking me in."

"Was your father away a lot?"

"He traveled for work. Some weeks he went away Sunday night and didn't return until Friday. Thing is . . . when he showed up, Mother changed completely. It was like I had disappeared. She focused on him and only him. He got her undivided attention. Before he came home, I was Mom's special little man. He'd walk in the door, and suddenly I'd be nothing."

"That would be very painful for a child," I said.

"It felt like she had been only pretending to love me."

"Your mother should have been able to love you in the presence of your father just like she did when he was gone."

"I know she loved me," Joel insisted. "She just couldn't show it when Father was there."

"You must have been really pissed at your father."

"No!"

"Jealous?"

"No. He was my father. Why would I be jealous of him? He traveled a lot. That was his job, his life. So what?"

"It was your life, too. Both your parents' attention should have been on you *and* each other, not on you *or* each other."

Accepting his jealousy and the way his parents had neglected him was not half so difficult for Joel as was the rest of what I had to tell him. "I think you've eroticized the pain you experienced as a child," I said. "You were left out of their marriage and wanted access to both of them. Your cuckolding fantasy is an exact imitation of how your parents treated you. The fantasy is a way for you to use the pleasure and oblivion of sex to blot out the pain."

"You're saying the couple in my fantasy are my parents? That's gross," he said.

"Fantasies are stories with themes and codes, like dreams. The couple in your fantasy represents your parents, and the story of the fantasy tells how you felt to be so left out.

"Your cuckolding fantasy was triggered when Sherri went on her internship. You assumed her attention was on the other guy and not on you anymore."

These various insights emerged over months as Joel progressed in his therapy. As we worked, he felt less compulsive with his porn. He felt no more need to meet couples. Still, he was lonely in his marriage, and so we talked about bringing Sherri into his therapeutic process.

NEGOTIATING AROUND A KINK

Joel was in my office, and he was feeling good.

"I want to bring Sherri here," he told me. "I've hated keeping all these secrets, but now I'm ready to tell her everything."

"I think that's great," I said, "but we need to have a plan of what you're going to tell her and how you tell her. You need to anticipate that she's going to react strongly, and you're going to feel attacked. At first, it may not go as well as you expect.

"Do you understand she will feel betrayed? What you tell her will be completely unexpected. You're going to need to have empathy for how she reacts, and that's going to be difficult, because she's going to be very angry with you. Even so, you will need to listen to her non-defensively."

"Well, I'll tell her about my cuckolding fantasy," Joel said. "How it turns me on and how it's like how my parents acted when I was a kid and how I'm not feeling compulsive anymore. I guess I could talk about her internship, too."

"What do you plan to tell her about what you've been doing?"

He paused and looked a little confused. "I guess I should tell her I've been doing the porn. Do you think I should tell her about meeting the couple?"

"You should tell her what you feel you need to tell her," I said. "Just remember, she hasn't been a part of your therapeutic process before now, so it's going to take her a while to understand what's going on for you the way you understand it. It will probably take her a while to find her empathy. Your empathy toward her has to come first. And don't forget, you can't just talk about your needs. She has needs, too. I imagine things don't look perfect from her perspective either."

* * *

They came to see me together the following week. Sherri looked way too cheerful, and I worried that Joel hadn't given her enough sense of what he planned to share with her. It was late afternoon, and they were both in their summer business attire: Joel in his short-sleeved shirt and tie, khaki pants, and work boots; Sherri in a green knit dress and black high-heeled pumps. As soon as they were seated, she took charge.

"Joel tells me you've been talking about his father and mother, how his father traveled a lot?" She looked from him to me. "He told me he was watching porn, which I already had a hunch about, but I didn't know it was a problem for him. This all has something to do with how he was raised?"

"The insights from our family-of-origin work are important," I said, "but maybe, Joel, we should start with what brought you to see me."

Joel told Sherri he was strongly drawn to a cuckolding fantasy and that he had come to see me because he was afraid he might be gay. Then I explained what cuckolding was.

"Dr. Kort thinks I've made real progress," Joel said, "and he's pretty sure I'm not gay."

I had warned him about overloading Sherri with too much new information too soon, but he either didn't understand or didn't agree, because the next thing he said was: "I met a couple for a cuckolding scene." Then, he explained a little bit about what that meant. Sherri, of course, was stunned.

"You're telling me you met a couple and had sex with them?" she said in a quiet, tightly controlled voice.

"No," Joel said, "I didn't have sex with them. I had a nonsexual fantasy that I fulfilled. Well, sort of nonsexual, I mean it turned me on, but I didn't have actual sex with either of them. I promise. I wasn't cheating."

"Then what did you do?" Sherri asked.

"I got ordered around. I was naked. They had sex and I watched. That's all."

"That's all!" Sherri said. "That's all! How do you expect me to believe that is all that happened? There must be more. Who meets people for sex and then doesn't have sex?"

"It was just a scene," Joel said.

"Are you crazy?" she said. "You think you can tell me that and I'll be, like, happy about it?"

She stood, crying, and headed for the door, but I managed to talk her out of leaving. "I know this is quite a shock," I told her. "It makes sense that you're upset. Who wouldn't be? Let me be here for you, too."

As she came back and sat down, I cautioned Joel that we were now going to listen to how she was feeling about it.

"How could you do this to me?" she told him. "Of course it was cheating. How could you endanger our marriage for a 'scene'? You've been lying to me. The porn is bad enough, sneaking off. . . . You know, I've been missing you, but now I think you should just get the hell out of my house."

And that's how the session went. She and Joel did agree to come back to see me the next day. I didn't think they should wait a week without further counseling.

My first concern was to validate Sherri's feelings. She was devastated. She felt so betrayed. All of Joel's sexual experimentation had been happening behind her back, and she had had no idea. Not to mention meeting the couple. She assumed Joel was gay, but when I assured her he wasn't, she said it didn't matter. She couldn't imagine staying married to him. Even so, she did agree that Joel didn't have to move out right away. They settled on separate bedrooms and minimal interactions at home for a while. (Chapter 10 focuses on the shock of discovering sexual secrets and gives a fuller sense of the process of healing from betrayal.)

After a half dozen sessions in which we mostly just listened to her and supported her, Joel gradually let her know he understood how hard this had hit her and how sorry he was. Eventually, he was able to give her more of his story, how his relationship with his parents had molded his fantasy. How Sherri's internship had triggered it.

As the shock of Joel's first confession passed, Sherri wanted things to "go back to normal." She told Joel, "No more porn in my house! No Internet sex. No meeting couples—or anyone else for that matter—for sex."

She wanted Joel to have no sexual experiences at all except with her. Joel pushed back. Maybe he felt he had the right, because he had "come clean" rather than "gotten caught."

"I'm glad everything is out in the open," he told her. "I know meeting with people for scenes was going too far. I was out of line there. But I don't see the problem with porn. It's not like I'm going to get AIDS over the Internet. Or make someone pregnant."

Sherri looked disgusted. Joel wasn't being very persuasive.

"I think this is easiest to understand," I said, "in terms of Joel's unmet needs. Having a porn outlet for his cuckolding fantasy is a way to soothe some of his unmet needs from the past."

"Well, what about my unmet needs?" Sherri asked. "I have a few of those. What's in it for me?"

So, we talked about what Sherri needed. She wanted Joel to be more available, more attentive, and more responsive. She had some specific ideas both for in the bedroom and out of it. She made sure Joel understood this wasn't just about him and his needs. He had to listen to her. He had to let her explain how she felt and what she wanted. He needed to understand that he had a long way to go to win her back.

I was blunt with them about their options: the alternative to an agreement was divorce, and either one of them could make the decision to part. Otherwise, some compromise was going to have to happen. I told Sherri, "Joel isn't going to agree to never watch porn. And what's good about that for you is that he doesn't want to agree to something he can't do, and he's no longer going to hide what he's doing. There's a kind of integrity in the way he doesn't want to lie to you. He's saying, 'This is who I am and I shouldn't have to hide it.' He doesn't want to have a secret sex life anymore."

I told Joel, "A few hours of porn a week is the most you can expect for your cuckolding fantasy, because Sherri isn't interested, and you guys need to put a lot more energy into being together. Sherri has suggested some nice ways you can connect, and you're going to be spending a lot of time in the future courting her again and regaining her trust. Her needs are going to come first for a while."

The negotiations between Joel and Sherri extended over several sessions. They were both stubborn and tenacious, but they did keep talking. Neither wanted a divorce. Joel agreed his porn would be limited to two hours a week. All the rest of his sex life would have to include Sherri. Sherri would get to plan one date a week in which Joel would "do things her way." They agreed in principle that they wanted to connect better and more often. They agreed that Joel had to re-earn Sherri's trust.

IT WASN'T ABOUT HER

I worked with Joel over the next year on his childhood, his loneliness, his jealousy, and his anger at his mother and father for abandoning him. His compulsivity became less intense as he was able to express his anger and sadness. Everybody has sexual interests. Joel's interest in cuckolding in itself wasn't a problem as he learned to make choices and keep boundaries. In time, Sherry was able to understand what his fantasy represented. She learned not to take it personally. It wasn't about her.

* * *

An interest in anal sex is so common it hardly even qualifies as a kink, but frequently I get an urgent phone call or e-mail from a woman with the "horrible revelation" that her allegedly straight husband would rather receive than give, as in the next chapter.

4

DAVID WANTS A KNOCK ON HIS BACK DOOR

Is He Gay?

It's pretty apparent that sexism, homophobia, and sex-negativity wind around each other like a braided rope that holds a lot of men back from exploring something that can bring amazing pleasure.

—Charlie Glickman, PhD[1]

Judith almost never woke up in the middle of the night, but she did this night. David wasn't in bed, and she heard the TV on, so she went downstairs. He was lying on the couch. It took her some moments to focus on what was in front of her. She'd never seen pornography herself, but she understood at once what David was watching. The screen flashed naked flesh, and the soundtrack moaned with nonstop simulated delight. She knew that men watched such things. She'd never thought about *David* doing it, but men had their peculiarities, and sometimes a woman understood to look away. But this she couldn't ignore.

She forced herself to look. On the screen a man was bent over and another was penetrating him from behind. On the couch, David was masturbating, but on his side. That looked odd. His right hand was doing the usual business, but the left was bent up behind him. She came closer. He was doing something with his butt.

He hadn't been very attentive to her lately, and she really was feeling neglected. Now this! She came closer, but she still couldn't see what he was doing, so she turned on the lights.

David leaped up. "Judy," he yelled. Something had been sticking out his rear, something that he was now holding. He ran into the kitchen with it. She went after him. There he was, naked, rubbing his hands on a paper towel.

"Well, I guess you surprised me," he said. "Let me just get my robe." And he returned to the family room.

"Surprised you doing what?" she asked, following him. "Where's that thing you were holding?"

"What thing?" he said, pulling on his robe and tying the belt.

He hadn't had much time to hide it. She went to the most likely place, the stainless steel kitchen trash can, and opened the lid to look in. There it was, a big solid black plastic dildo.

"What's this?" she said and leaned forward.

"Don't touch it," he said, coming over and closing the lid. "I'll take care of it."

She walked back to the family room. The movie was still playing. Men were getting it up the rear. So, this was sodomy! The nuns at school had warned about this. Her first reaction was a kind of disappointment. It should have looked more wicked. Really, it looked sort of silly.

David had been streaming to the TV from his laptop, but now he reached over and closed the window. He went back to the kitchen, and Judith took advantage of his absence to check his Web history. This had been "Nasty Raw Bareback," and before that "Strap Attack." David returned.

"Okay, David," she said. "Talk to me. How could you? The children might have come down and found you."

David was blushing, but he wasn't talking.

"You were watching homosexual pornography," Judith said, "And were you pushing that thing in your . . . ," but she couldn't say it.

"I took care of that," he said. Then, he just stood there, looking mortified.

"Are you one of them?" she asked. He shook his head "no," but he wouldn't offer any explanation. She asked him a dozen questions after that. She told him a thing or two about what a miserable sneak he was, but he wouldn't argue and he wouldn't explain. He waited her out until they were both exhausted. Two days later they were in my office.

IS ANAL SEX GAY?

David was wearing a suit and tie. Judith had on a dress with pearls and heels. These people were *respectable*, and they wanted me to know it.

"He won't talk to me," Judith began. "I caught him watching homosexual pornography, but he says he's not a homosexual."

I turned to David. He certainly was blushing like a man who had been caught in the act, but he wasn't defending himself or explaining. I went back to Judith.

"Maybe you should tell me what happened," I suggested.

"I think he should tell you," she said, nervously opening and closing her purse.

"David, can you get us started here?" I asked him. His eyes were wide, and he'd gone pale. He didn't say anything.

"Judith," I said, "would you mind going to the waiting room? Maybe David would be more comfortable talking just with me for now."

After she was gone, David did look more relaxed.

"Can you tell me what's going through your head right now?" I asked.

"It's difficult to talk about," he admitted, looking at his hands. "I don't think I'm gay. It was just bad timing, Judith coming in like that. Most of my porn is pegging.

Pegging—A sexual practice in which a woman penetrates a man's anus with a strap-on dildo.

"I've been into anal ever since I was twelve," he told me. "I would finger myself in the tub; it felt good. Later, it was vegetables. Squash, carrots, cucumbers with Vaseline or butter. Then, when I was fourteen somebody showed me some gay porn, you know, anal stuff, like what Judith caught me with, and I was fascinated. I worried I might be gay, but I couldn't talk to anyone about it. I watched what turned me on, and for a long time that was gay porn. Then, later I found strap-on porn, and that sent me over the moon. Pegging's what I really like."

"Judith thinks you're gay."

"I don't blame her, what she found me watching."

"Are you attracted to the guys?"

"No. I've never been into the guys," he told me. "I always fast forward to the fucking. I like the sex. I have thought about a guy fucking me," he admitted. "Does that make me gay? I don't know much about being gay."

"It hinges mainly on how you see other men," I told him. "Would it be okay if I asked you some questions about that?"

I went through my usual screening. He was not in the least gay or bi. His focus on anal sex seemed to be the whole story. I tried to find out why this had become such an issue in their marriage.

"Did you ever discuss anal sex with Judith?" I asked him.

"I let her know I was interested, but you know . . . she's religious. It's sodomy as far as she's concerned."

"She seemed pretty unprepared for what she discovered when she came downstairs and found you."

"I didn't exactly tell her I was doing it on my own."

"But you told her you were interested?"

"Not in so many words."

"Well, I think you should tell her. I think you need to be direct."

"But then she'll be sure I'm gay."

"I'll help her understand that you're not."

I actually met two more times with David alone. He was terrified of facing Judith and telling her everything, so we worked on his shame. I reviewed with him how normal it is for a straight man to be turned on by anal sex. Then, he insisted that I do a session with Judith alone "to make sure she's prepared."

A MAN BENT OVER ISN'T A MAN

When I met with Judith, it had been nearly a month since our first meeting. She'd had time to get over her surprise, and she was relieved that I could confirm that David wasn't gay. She had done her own research and now understood that it was common for a heterosexual man to like to be stimulated anally. She was less frightened about her marriage and less concerned that David was into something harmful.

David still wasn't being very open with her, so I took it upon myself to explain about strap-ons and strap-on porn. I told her that many straight men enjoy at least the fantasy of pegging.

"The nuns taught us that sodomy is disgusting," Judith said. "I guess the idea is that it's something gays do, and since homosexuality is a sin . . ."

"In fact, some gay men never do it," I pointed out.

"Well, when I was a child," she said, "of course, I believed everything they told me. Then, my best friend let me know that she and her husband do it that way, so she won't get pregnant anymore. Opened my eyes."

"Does it seem different if the woman's doing it to the man?"

"I think a man should be a man in the bedroom," she told me.

I'd heard this before. The issue is whether having anal sex on the receiving end means you're not masculine. I couldn't resolve it with her entirely in one individual session. She was willing to accept that anal wasn't gay, but she had always believed that the man should be giving and not receiving. I hoped we could change her mind. It was harming their marriage that David thought he had to hide so much of his sexuality from her.

ASKING FOR IT

I met with David and Judith about ten times together or separately. Judith learned to be less intimidated, less insulted, by David's interest in anal sex. She began to understand that it wasn't a threat to their marriage and it was important to him. David's shame was turning out to be the more persistent stumbling block. This therapy wasn't just about informing Judith; it was about bringing the two of them together in a constructive dialogue. Judith didn't seem to have trouble expressing herself to him, but he was struggling.

One of our later sessions was a breakthrough. I'd been asking David to explain to Judith his lifelong interest in anal, and he had done so in bits and pieces. That day I pressed him to go further. "You've always kept your anal sex separate, a part of your masturbation, but you've also told me you'd like to include Judith, haven't you?"

"I've asked her," David admitted, "but I understand that she doesn't want to. It isn't her thing."

"Asked me what?" Judith interrupted. "You haven't asked me any-thing."

David gaped at her. I took up the thread. "Would you like me to say it for you?" I asked him. He shook his head *yes*. "Well," I said to her, "David likes the way it feels to be touched on his anus, and to be penetrat-ed, with lube, and with his dildos and vibrators. He likes the way it feels physically, and he likes the way it makes him feel emotionally."

"And he'd like me to do what?"

"Ask David," I suggested.

"What would you like me to do?" she said to David.

David was pale with fear, but he let me lead him. "Your core fantasy," I said to him. "You've told me. Can you tell Judith?"

"My core fantasy," he said to her, "is that you learn to use a strap on . . . and use it on me." Without pausing he went on. "Look. It's all right. I don't need you to do it. If you don't do it, it's fine. I can live without it."

"Well, that's nice," Judith said. "I appreciate your saying that, but I'd like to try it for you."

His astonishment was indescribable.

"I've been thinking it over," Judith said. "At first, I thought you shouldn't want this. I thought it had something to do with homosexuality and took you away from me. But now I see it isn't about me at all. It's something for you. I want to try to do it. I'm not sure I'll get into it, but I want to try. I want to please you."

"You can start in small ways," I pointed out. "Just watch what David does for himself at first."

David's eyes were moist. "But doesn't your Bible tell you that you can't do this?" he asked her.

She paused a moment, then spoke with a measured emphasis. "*My Bible*," she said, looking at him calmly, "lets me do whatever I want to do with my husband."

She turned to me. "It won't be easy," she conceded. "You have to understand that I was raised to be a lady. Doing the things he wants me to do is going to be hard. It goes against everything I ever learned about being passive and being 'nice.' That doesn't mean I can't do them. It's sexy for him, and it probably could be sexy for me." She turned to him. "Doing this is going to go against my training, my upbringing, but so what? I want you to be happy. I'm with you. I'm on your side."

I looked over at David, and he was crying. Crying like a baby. Judith moved over to hold him, and that's the way the session ended.

IS ANAL SEX A PROBLEM?

Maybe you're thinking: *I can't believe anal sex could be such an issue in the twenty-first century.* What can I say? Men and women come into my office or e-mail me regularly, worried that a man who likes to receive anal can't be a real, masculine man.

Two prejudices are operating here. Sometimes giving anal is a trigger for a straight man to think he's gay, but not usually. He stops worrying when he learns that lots of straight men want to give anal to a woman. But if he wants to receive, then the prejudice is "that's gay," which is plain and simple homophobia. It isn't true.

The other prejudice is a kind of figment of patriarchy, the idea that the man should always be "on top." I've interviewed so many women in my office who wanted equality for women in everything but sex. "In the bedroom I need you to take charge," she'll tell her man, "but don't you dare push your weight around outside of it." But why does the man always have to be on top and penetrating? Can't he just as well be soft and penetrated? The woman who realizes and accepts that possibility will be making herself and her man happy in ways she might never have dreamed of.

This book is not a sex manual, but a number of good books on enjoying anal sex are available, including *Anal Pleasure and Health: A Guide for Men, Women and Couples*[2] and *The Adventurous Couple's Guide to Strap-On Sex*.[3] Enjoy or choose not to enjoy, but remember: An attraction to anal sex is not a psychological problem.

LOVING IT

I advised Judith and David on how to familiarize Judith with anal sex in baby steps: watch him doing it to himself, read a book or view an instructional video, watch the porn (or not), use a toy on David but not as a strap-on. Then, they could choose to experiment with the fully dominant penetrating woman.

As Judith and David practiced, her resistance quickly evaporated. There isn't any subtle way to put the end of the story of David and Judith. She loved doing him. Like most women who try this, she was surprised how aroused and "wet" it made her to be in a top and dominant role with her husband.

* * *

Sometimes a partner's kink can be shared. Sometimes it doesn't need to be shared, but it's still not a problem for the couple. But sometimes a kink becomes virtually an identity for a partner, and a difference in identity can stress the couple just as much as a difference in sexual orientation. In the next chapter, we consider a couple whose marriage is threatened by such a difference.

5

ADAM MUST BE THE MASTER

BDSM as an Identity

Sticks and stones may break my bones, but chains and whips excite me.

—Rihanna[1]

Adam was whipping Daniel's ass with a belt. Each snap of the leather brought a gasp of pain, but Daniel wasn't using his safe word. Adam found himself both concerned for Daniel and touched that he was giving him the gift of such suffering. Adam knew that when submissives were "in the zone" they sometimes forgot their safe words or even forgot they were in a scene, but Daniel seemed aware.

> *Safe Word*—Because BDSM play can include insincere calls by the "victim" to stop, a special word that means "stop" is agreed upon ahead of time that is unlikely to be said at random, for example, "wombat."

"Had enough, slave?" Adam asked, staying in character as the sadistic master but giving Daniel a chance to opt out.

There was a pause. Then Daniel said, sounding both submissive and mocking at the same time, "My master decides how much I suffer. It's not for me to say."

Adam gave him another crack with the belt. Daniel wasn't just playacting; his gasp came from real pain. Adam had never had a submissive take this much punishment. Of course, Daniel was his first man. It made sense he could take more. Compared to this, the women only allowed him a dozen or so stings, and maybe some crying, and after that the hugs, the "better now" reconciliation that ended most scenes for Adam.

> *BDSM*—Bondage, discipline, sadism, and masochism refers to sexual stimulation by playing with various themes of exaggerated hierarchy. These days, BDSM is a well-organized community with its own rules and customs, educational materials, and activities. B&D and S&M can be used loosely as synonyms for BDSM or refer to components including intense physical sensations (spanking, paddling, whipping, etc.). The phrase "dominance and submission" is used sometimes to emphasize the more psychological aspects of this play.

> *Scene*—In BDSM play, it is an interaction between two or more people, like a scene in a movie, in which a BDSM encounter is acted out.

> *Master, Dominant; Slave, Submissive*—Terms indicating the roles to be played by individuals in a BDSM scene or gathering.

A scene was never followed by sex, at least not for Adam, even when he played with a woman. He was a married man, and he took that seriously. He'd had sex with Cynthia when she'd been active, of course, but she was his wife. Adam was a man who could keep boundaries, and BDSM play wasn't about sex for him anyway. It was sexual, but he didn't need to fuck his slaves. Of course, he didn't think he was gay, and he didn't think he wanted to have sex with Daniel, but something amazing was happening just the same.

Daniel squirmed on the bed, and Adam gave him another smack. "You stay still, you miserable fuckup. You stay there until I say you can move. Understand?"

"Yes, master," came the meek reply.

God, thought Adam. *This has been going on for a long time.* Then he had a sudden rush of insight. He started trembling and put down the belt.

Daniel's not going to use his safe word. I could beat him bloody. He would let me. It's an offering of his pain to me, his trust. I love this.

Adam let Daniel lie there for a while, but he was through beating him. He didn't want to really hurt him. What a wonderful thing it was to have someone give himself that way. It made Adam feel protective. It wasn't love. He hardly knew Daniel, but it was like love, the way you feel with a tiny baby, feeling its vulnerability, how totally it depends on you.

Adam had been doing scenes as a master for almost two decades in the local BDSM community, but he'd never experienced anything like this before.

* * *

Adam came home late, filled with excitement, but also confusion. *Something had happened tonight, but what?* He was glad for once that Cynthia wasn't waiting up for him. He needed time to think and process the amazing experience he had just shared with a man he barely knew. He paused in the foyer and looked in the mirror: He loved his "second skin," black leather shirt, vest, and pants, and those big boots, which had been his first fetish purchase. He and Cynthia had gone together to Noir Leather, a local S&M sex shop, and picked them out. He had been really nervous about "outing" his S&M side to her. Now, as he looked at himself with his shaved head and tattoos and all the rest, he had to smile, remembering how he'd trembled to share that first purchase with Cynthia. It had been some kind of coming out for him. He had been claiming a part of himself, a part of himself he was claiming still.

In those days Cynthia had been more willing to participate in his BDSM interests. She'd been a new twenty-year-old bride and ready for anything. She let him spank her a little and tie her up and drip honey on her and lick it off. She'd thought that was fun. She'd gone to the local BDSM gatherings, the technique demonstrations, education classes, and play parties. It had all seemed a little silly to her but not nasty or anything. Nobody was pushy. Funny to think that people would be so respectful in an S&M group, but that was the way it was, and it allowed her to hang out and let Adam get into it. It was her gift to him.

> *Play Party*—A gathering where various BDSM activities are demonstrated or acted out.

By the time their second child came, she didn't want to take part in gatherings anymore, so they had agreed to let Adam continue alone. It had always meant a lot more to him than it had to her, and she knew enough by then not to worry that he was into something horrible.

Now, though, Adam felt a thrill of dread. Tonight had been different. It hadn't been a regular play party. He'd met Daniel at a hotel, just the two of them. And okay . . . he'd played with a man, and Adam had always played with women before, but that wasn't the shocking part. The shocking part was how deeply Adam was moved. How he felt his life had changed.

So, what did it mean? Was he gay? That was one possible conclusion, but he wasn't so sure. He didn't feel gay.

He'd never hid anything from Cynthia before, but he didn't want to share this with her. Not yet. He needed to sort it out first for himself.

A PILLAR OF THE COMMUNITY

Adam came to see me in a rather elegant blue suit and tie. He was a leader in the local business community, but, of course, he'd come to see me about the more hidden side of his life.

He had just told me about his cathartic experience with Daniel, and he wanted me to help him understand what had happened. Of course, he also wanted my opinion about his "gayness," and he was struggling with how to tell his wife he'd been playing BDSM games with a man.

He wasn't worried about being into BDSM. "What's got me worried is I played with a man, which I've never done before. I'm really just into women, but I *loved* playing with this guy."

"So, how did you come to play with a guy in the first place?" I asked.

"That's a long story."

"Okay, maybe you should start at the beginning."

"I've been doing this stuff since I was little," he told me. "When I was in the sixth grade, I'd daydream about having a naked girl under my control. I'd tie her up and tease her. In the daydream I wouldn't hurt her, but she'd be afraid of what I was going to do, and I loved the thrill of her fear and her embarrassment at being naked. It turned me on. Maybe I should say, in case you're worried that you've got a sex criminal on your hands, that it never even occurred to me to do anything to a real girl.

"I'd look up key words in the dictionary like 'spanking' and 'discipline,' and, of course, whenever a guy would spank his girlfriend in the movies or television, or someone would be tied up, I'd be fascinated. After I discovered *Penthouse* and *Penthouse Forum* and especially their sister publication, *Variations*, I finally realized I wasn't alone, that lots of people were turned on by kinky stuff.

"When I was dating Cynthia, she won my heart by letting me spank her. I wouldn't do it hard, and she'd giggle her head off, but it was important to me, and she didn't seem to mind. When I'd tie her to the bed and touch her all over and make her wait before she came, she would go wild.

"I discovered Noir Leather in Royal Oak and, by reading their bulletin board, got into local groups like The Chateau, The Spanking Needs Forum, and The Michigan BDSM Social Club. Then, on the Internet, Southeast Michigan Adult Gatherings and others.

"After Cynthia and I got married, she knew how important BDSM was for me, so she agreed to go with me to S&M meetings and demonstrations. It wasn't a big deal for her, at least while we were in our twenties and before our first child. Then we both got kind of busy, and it was hard even for me to find time to build my business and socialize with the S&M crowd at the same time. Still, it was very important for me to gather with 'my people' and for Cynthia to go along. I didn't want to be one of those lonely kinky single guys trying to find a girl who would let him dominate her. I mean, vanilla dating's hard enough, and I felt lucky to have found Cynthia."

"So she'd go with you to these gatherings . . ."

"There are all kinds of gatherings. Some, you just meet people and have dinner. A public restaurant, no kinky dress or behavior to scare the vanilla people. Then, some gatherings are demonstrations, but people can wear their favorite BDSM costumes if they want to. A demonstration is educational, you know: A couple will show the safe way to do flogging or hot wax or medical play. Something like that. Then, there are the parties, where there is more out-and-out play. You might bring your girl and spank her, or find a girl there and spank her. 'All safe, sane, and consensual,' of course. These groups get rid of the crazies quick. In fact, I've never met any crazies in all the years I've been doing BDSM. These are very considerate people. Everybody is so clear about limits and boundaries and safe words. The more experienced players know the newbies will try to go too far if you let them, and we protect them from themselves."

Safe, Sane, and Consensual—A general statement of rules governing BDSM play.

Vanilla—A term used in the BDSM community for people or activities not into BDSM.

"You've told me you don't have sex at play parties. Doesn't it turn you on to spank a girl you meet at a party?"

"Of course it turns me on. All this turns me on. But I don't need to fuck the ladies I spank. We always agree ahead of time: no intercourse, no sexual contact. If I come home horny, Cynthia's cool with it. If it's been 'one of those days' for her, then I'm left to take care of myself, but more often than not, she's glad there's still a place for loving between us."

"So it's a sexual experience without sexual contact?"

"That's one way of saying it. I'm touching the girl's bottom, and there's a lot of skin on skin in that, but there's a line we don't cross. Hard to believe maybe, but that's the way it happens.

"Cynthia is satisfied I'm not being unfaithful. She's seen everything. She knows what we do at the parties. But now with this Daniel, I'm not so sure how she'll react."

"Because Daniel's a guy? And you think Cynthia might have a strong reaction?"

"It's my strong reaction to Daniel. That's what's really different here. I think she'll freak out. Maybe she'll think I'm gay. Maybe she'll just think I've lost my mind. To tell you the truth, I'm a little freaked out myself."

"You said you always played with women?"

"Daniel tricked me," Adam said.

"Tell me about it."

"It happened like this: Most of the available women I meet at the parties—very nice ladies, fun, friendly—want it soft, and I want it hard. I've asked around, and I've checked online. I've posted queries on some local blogs to see if any women would like to try it hard the way I want, and finally someone e-mailed me from The Chateau's Facebook page. 'Deirdre' said she was an unattached lady, looking for someone who could give her hard spankings.

"I was so excited by this. We negotiated by e-mail how it would go: safe words, hard limits, implements. She wanted straps and switches but not canes or whips. She talked about how she wanted to be submissive, ordered around, verbally degraded, made to wait for it, made to take it. She understood that I was married; no sex was okay. She just wanted the scene, the experience of extended domination and the feel of being soundly beaten.

"I was getting very excited by these e-mails," Adam admitted. "I love Cynthia, but she never let me do it hard. I always respected her limits, of course, and her limits were hardly more than a few lovers' smacks and a little silly bondage."

"So, what happened with Deidre?" I prompted.

"We set up a meeting at a regular Chateau party, so it would be safe and open and everything. I should have been suspicious right then, because she said she was a member, but I'd never heard of her. Anyway, the day before we were to meet, she confessed via e-mail that she wasn't a woman but a guy. I was so disappointed! And angry! I told him to fuck off, and I blocked him from my e-mail."

"So then what happened?"

"Deidre's e-mails had gotten me so excited! I loved what she/he had told me she/he wanted to do. I found myself thinking a lot about it. Finally, I unblocked him, and we e-mailed some more. He apologized. He begged me to give him a chance. He said he would do anything."

"Was he gay?"

"Maybe. He had to be. I didn't ask. We met at a restaurant, not at one of the parties. I didn't want any of the regulars to see me playing with a guy."

"So guys don't play together at these parties?"

"It's tricky the way that works. The group is technically gay friendly, but in practice not really. A master will play with a male slave if his mistress is there. Somehow, a guy needs his woman to "de-gay" him."

"That sounds pretty homophobic," I said, "but tell me about Daniel."

"He's younger than I am, in his twenties I guess, and he seemed nice enough. He confirmed everything he had told me, except of course his name was Daniel, not Deidre. He told me I could call him Deidre. He said he would dress like a girl for me. He was desperate to play, and I liked that.

"He told me he'd done BDSM with gay men before but that he had a particular desire to have a straight guy dominate and humiliate him. I asked him why he e-mailed *me*, and he said he had e-mailed many other straight male masters, and I was the first who was willing to meet him.

"We went to a nearby hotel. I made him strip and crawl around on the floor, licking my boots and eventually I whipped his ass with my belt until he was gasping with every sting. Even so, I wasn't prepared to go very far on a first meeting. Did he really know what he was getting into? I whipped him for maybe ten minutes. We had a safe word that he never used. We spent the rest of the hour together, just me sitting and him kneeling at my feet, and he seemed content and not seriously hurt, and so that was the first time we met."

"How did you feel about it?" I asked him.

"Daniel/Deidre wasn't a girl," Adam said, "and I wished he had been, but what I discovered was that in some sense it didn't really matter. He was a person willing to do the things with me I had wanted to do for so long. It felt completely different, satisfying at a much deeper level. I can't explain it. That's just how it worked out.

"I met him three more times for longer and longer scenes, and that last time, when he wouldn't use his safe word, when I realized that he was putting himself in my hands totally, something just happened in me different from what I've ever experienced before. He was giving himself to me completely; that trust brought me into the scene in a completely new way."

Adam paused. He was clearly very moved. I waited to see if he wanted to say more. Finally, he went on. "It was *profound*. That's the word that comes to me. It's about who I am. Daniel is a nice play partner, but . . . he's a guy, and *that let me see it wasn't about sex.*"

"I'm only into women; that hasn't changed. This was much more about who I am than about being turned on. I got it. It didn't matter, woman or man, just somebody totally mine, who was willing to suffer as long as I wanted him to. He really put himself in my hands. That was . . . amazing."

> "The longing for validation can motivate people to overcome strict upbringings, banish guilt and shame, and find camaraderie. It can push them to find or create space where those desires won't be judged, but instead shared. It can be an incredible relief to know you're not 'the only one' with your particular 'kink.'"*
>
> *Mollena Williams, "Be Careful Not to Criminalize Fantasies," *New York Times*, March 5, 2013.

After Adam's long personal statement, I went through my standard clinical assessment to measure the extent of his gay orientation. On the beach test, he came out straight. He hadn't experienced any particular youthful noticing of males in his adolescence. He wasn't homophobic the way repressed gay men can be. He wanted to wake up in the morning in the arms of a woman—his wife—and not a man.

As for Daniel, Adam was not attracted to him or his body. Playing with Daniel was Adam's unique opportunity to have a pure BDSM experience, to express his core BDSM nature. And that's really what had so shaken him.

Adam and I met for a number of sessions. As Adam reconciled himself to his deeper identity with his BDSM persona, the issue of how to tell his wife remained unresolved. There seemed no better solution than to invite Cynthia to come to my office and let Adam explain everything to her there.

MORE ON BDSM

Most people are turned on by mild BDSM sex play, a smack to the bottom during an embrace, the holding of hands above the head during a kiss. However, for some people BDSM, dominance and submission, spanking, or some other element of sexual control becomes so important to their lives that it is more properly like an identity than it is like a sexual preference. These people feel the need to socialize, to be affirmed by like-minded people. They have to claim themselves: *I'm okay; you're okay.*

We're not crazy, and we're nice people, too. Coming out as a lifestyle BDSM practitioner is similar to coming out gay. It has the central stigma. It has the sexual secrecy. It has its own culture. And it may be arguably even more taboo in society at large.

When a person's core sexual scripts are strongly laced with BDSM themes, these themes will be with that person for all of his or her life. The person will continue to be turned on by BDSM, and that will never change. Whether people choose to downplay or overtly express "what turns them on" will vary according to personality and circumstance. Also, "sexual themes" often play out in a person's spiritual expressions, creative activities, or social relationships without being explicitly sexual in the ordinary sense.

I'm often asked where BSDM kinks come from, and despite many theories, the practical answer is that nobody knows. It touches on broader currents in psychology and society, and many experts believe a tendency toward BDSM is there in everyone. It emerges as more significant in some people for unknown reasons.

I should note that a sexual interest is BDSM is rarely associated with criminal activities or atrocities, but the media love a crime story that includes BDSM elements. This gives the impression that BDSM and crime always go together, and that is false. There have been legislative attempts to try to make all S&M literature and activities criminal, which is absurd and unnecessary.

The field of psychology has a history of seeing BDSM as pathological. I've heard therapists say that BDSM is merely an adult response to childhood trauma. "Sex should never be about pain or suffering; it should be only about joy and pleasure." This doesn't take into account that for many people pain and pleasure are mixed together, and suffering can be eroticized in healthy ways. No creditable scientific study has shown any trend of psychological pathologies in people drawn to BDSM. In fact, BDSM activities recently have been removed as "disorders" from the *Diagnostic and Statistical Manual*[2] used for diagnosing mental disorders. (See a longer discussion of this topic in chapter 12.) Although it is true that many people who have BDSM desires are troubled by them, this is often because of the shame they have been taught to feel about their atypical fantasies. Safe, sane, and consensual sex of any kind cannot logically or humanely be called criminal or pathological.[3]

Perhaps the most popular mainstream book with a strong BDSM theme to date has been *Fifty Shades of Grey* by E. L. James (pseudonym of Erika Leonard), where the lead character, Mr. Grey, a closeted dominant heavily into BDSM, finds Ana to be a willing participant in fulfilling his BDSM desires. This book's popularity has helped destigmatize BDSM. It's difficult to imagine the media making a big deal of finding this book on a serial murderer's bookshelf, although in the past pundits have made much of associating S&M porn with violent crime.

Playing safely with BDSM requires well-developed relational skills and maturity. It involves trust, cooperation, communication, and vulnerability by both master and slave. All this is illustrated in *Fifty Shades of Grey*. For those who enjoy BDSM, their activities bring excitement and pleasure just like any other fantasy-based sex play.

ADAM AND CYNTHIA TOGETHER

It was winter, and Cynthia kept on her coat. She sat in a chair; Adam took the couch. She wore jeans and practical boots; Adam wore one of the suits I usually saw him in, with rubber overshoes to acknowledge the weather.

Adam explained about his encounter with Daniel and his concern about his own reactions, how he'd worked with me to clear his confusion and understand what he'd gone through. He also said he was anxious about sharing with Cynthia. He wanted her to understand. He was worried she'd be upset.

When Adam was finished, Cynthia seemed a little stunned. "I had no idea you were meeting people in hotels."

"Just Daniel. Just four times."

"You never used to play with guys," she said.

"I explained about that. I'm not gay."

"I think I know by now you aren't gay," Cynthia said, "but are you going to see him again?"

"Maybe," Adam admitted. "I've never found a girl who would let me play that hard. Daniel wants to suffer just as much as I want him to."

"You're scaring me," Cynthia said. "You sound like a sadist. Not a play-party sadist. A real sadist."

"It is sadistic," Adam agreed, "and maybe you could say I'm a sadist, if that means this stuff is deep in me. I'm more of a sadist than we thought, but I'm not a monster. I don't want to really hurt Daniel or anybody. I want to give him what he wants that fits what I want. He was in my power, wanting to be in my power. I could do anything to him, but I wouldn't make him go beyond what he could take, and he trusted me not to. Don't you see how wonderful that was for me?"

"I thought you were just going to play parties," Cynthia said, "I mean, with our friends in the community, like Sally and Penny. Every time I turned around one of those girls would be over your lap with her panties pulled down, but there wasn't any harm in that. Now this?"

"Well, you're right. This is different. Playing with Daniel has opened up a whole new world about what BDSM means to me. That last time, he was waiting for me to decide what was enough for him. We'd been at it almost an hour. He was naked and cuffed at the foot of the bed, and I finally understood how important it was to me to hold someone's fate like that, to have him be completely subject to me."

"Well," said Cynthia, "I think I've been a pretty good sport about all this."

"You've been great," said Adam, and his tone was sincere, "but this is something different. It's about who I am."

"So now what?" Cynthia asked, looking very unhappy.

"You know," Adam said, his eyes glowing, "it's been hard for me to understand, but now I know I'm more into this than I thought. It's not just a sex fantasy. It's not just play. I used to make fun of the 'lifestyle' couples, but now I think . . . well, that makes sense to me. A way of life. I understand it now. I want it."

"Why don't you come back with me into the community?" Adam said to Cynthia. "You haven't been with us for a few years, but didn't you used to enjoy it?"

"It was fun for a while, but now I don't have the time," Cynthia said. "I've got children to raise, and the time for these games should be over for you, too. You're taking it way too seriously. You've got to quit before it makes you crazy."

Adam looked to me for help.

"Adam is coming out," I explained, "not as a gay man, but as someone's whose identity is BDSM. I've seen this before," I said, hoping that might reassure her. "Adam is one of those individuals who need BDSM more as a way of being in the world than as just a sexual expression. The fact that Adam was so exhilarated and excited wasn't about Daniel. It certainly wasn't about being gay. It was about Adam finding himself."

Cynthia was only half listening. "I want you to be done with this stuff," she said to Adam. "All of it. I think you should throw away all those leather costumes and let your hair grow back and stop trying to look like such a tough guy. This has gone too far. I should have said *no* long ago. I don't want you off doing anything with anybody: boy or girl, it doesn't matter. I never dreamed you'd get so . . . up to your neck in it. I thought it was just play. Just letting off steam."

The grief in Adam's face was hard to bear. "I've found something wonderful," he said. "I love you. I want us to stay together. But don't you understand? This is who I am."

"I love you, too," Cynthia said. Her own grief was bringing her to tears. "I understand how important this is to you."

"But I can't have you off on Fantasy Island when I need you with me. You've got to choose. This 'play' is maybe all you want in life, but it can't be my life." She was crying now.

"I need you to come back to me and your children," she said.

"God," said Adam, impatient, pleading. "It's not all I want in life. I want you. I want the children. Think of BDSM as a job. My new job. Not more important than you and the children. Never that. But important enough that I can't give it up."

"I'm so sorry, Adam," Cynthia said. "You have to give it up . . . or give us up. I can't stand it anymore."

HOW COULD BDSM BE THAT IMPORTANT?

Cynthia and Adam divorced. Their fifteen-year marriage ended. Adam wanted to stay married, he wanted to be there for his children, but he could not give up his BDSM activities. Cynthia couldn't remain the wife of a BDSM master. Why was it this difficult?

I think it's wrong to look at Adam and Cynthia's story only through the lens of sexual preference and satisfaction. One of the problems with understanding situations when there's a sexual element is that inevitably the sex is given the most emphasis, no matter what else is going on. The issue for Adam is identity. He doesn't meet with his friends in the BDSM community for sexual release. He meets with them to affirm who he is.

When does a sexual theme, an element of a core sexual script, emerge into identity? I can't answer that question. I just know that sometimes it does, and when that happens, something deeper than "mere sex" is happening. The identity has revealed the sexual interest, or has been revealed by it, but the identity is not the same as the sexual interest.

A few years after Adam and Cynthia divorced, Adam came back to consult with me. He's semiretired and spending more and more of his time as a leader in the BDSM communities in Detroit and Chicago. He feels he's making an important contribution. He feels it has given new meaning to his life. He and Cynthia are coparenting their two children.

"It took a while," he told me, "but she finally understood. See, she thought it was all about kinky sex, and my preference for something sexual took precedence over her and the children, and she just couldn't put the pieces together. After she understood it was about who I am at my core, she was okay with it. She could let me go."

* * *

In the next chapter, Carlos fears he may be gay, but he's never acted on his gay inclinations. Anna loves him and wants them to marry. Should they wait and see if Carlos is coming out, or go ahead and get married?

6

CARLOS'S ANXIETY

Men Who Obsess about Being Gay

I have sometimes wondered if those who experience the most distress from such thoughts as these do so because they were raised with more strongly homophobic or anti-gay attitudes to begin with . . .

—Fred Pensel[1]

Paganini Pizza in Ferndale, Michigan, was a small Italian restaurant where locals could drop by at all hours for coffee or a glass of Chianti. It had been popular for decades with off-duty cops and workers who'd finished their shifts but didn't want to go home or hang out in a bar. Carlos had chosen it for his meeting with his fiancée, Anna, because people mind their own business there. He wanted to be able to talk with Anna without having to worry about being overheard. He hated it when people stared at him, tried to listen in, or talked about him behind his back. He had to try to keep focused on what he wanted to tell Anna.

Anna came in stamping the snow off her boots, gave Carlos the smile he loved, then had a quick word with the owner, Maria. Carlos knew that she was ordering peppermint tea. She always ordered peppermint tea. That was good. Peppermint tea would help her stay calm.

"How was your shift?" Anna asked as she sat down. He had told her he wanted to share something important, but she thought it wouldn't be polite to get down to "business" right away, even though she was dying to hear what he had to say.

He shrugged and gave her a tired grin. "Nobody yelled at me, and I got paid. Could have been worse.

"Snow looks bad for driving," he added, taking a sip of his coffee. It was 4 p.m., but he drank strong coffee all the time.

"Not that bad for February," she said, shaking her long black hair free of her stocking cap. "Are you mad at me?" she said. "I'm dying to know what couldn't wait."

"Sorry," Carlos said. "No, of course I'm not mad at you. Of course, I'm not. But I've been worrying about something, and I've kept it from you. I didn't want to bother you with it. It hurts my heart to face this, but I have to. It would hurt worse in the long run not to. You know, Anna, how much I love you?"

"You're not calling off the engagement, are you? Just because I wanted us to set a date for the wedding?" She tried to make it sound playful, but he could see real fear in her eyes.

"No," he said. "I'm not calling off anything. I just need to tell you, to not keep anything from you. I don't usually talk about what goes on in my head. Hard to do, you know?"

Anna nodded. She didn't know, but she could see how difficult this was for him.

"I'm not sure I've ever let myself talk about this. I just figured most guys worried about it, but in high school I sure wasn't going to talk about it."

She nodded and tried to smile. He went on.

"It really never occurred to me I might be anything like gay." Carlos paused to check Anna's reaction, but she had gone neutral—listening, sipping her tea, and nodding. She wasn't having the Big Reaction Carlos was afraid of. At least, not yet.

"I mean, people kid around, but nobody talks about it. I mean Peter in the toolroom is gay. Everybody knows he is, and that's okay, but nobody talks about it either. I've always been into girls, but then one day I just started worrying I might be gay. I don't know what happened. I just started worrying about it."

"Are you trying to tell me you're gay?" Anna interrupted. Carlos could see her eyes misting over.

"No," he said quickly. "Not exactly. Please, listen. It's just that you know how strict my parents are. I've always tried to be a good boy, make them proud of me."

"They are proud of you," Anna said, "and so am I."

"My parents would kill me if they thought I was gay. It's gotten to the point that I worry about worrying. Sometimes I come off my shift, and it's been difficult, and I want to unwind, and the only thing I can think of is maybe watching some gay porn, to see if it turns me on. So I watch, and I'm not turned on, but I still worry. The next time I need to unwind, I do it again."

Now Anna was looking worried. Carlos quickly went on. "I've always wanted my own family more than anything, but since I fell in love with you, I don't want *a family* anymore—I want *our family*. I can't imagine anything else. I don't usually go in for stuff like 'soul mates,' but . . . what can I say? You're my soul mate, and I can't imagine a future without you. I don't want to lose you. But what if I really am gay, what then for us?

"I mean, we are wonderful for each other and meant for each other. You won't let me get away with anything. You make me a better person. You're the best person in the world. Your smile is the most beautiful thing I know. I live to see that smile. God has brought us together in a way that I didn't even know was possible, and I feel blessed every day for that. I love every minute I'm with you, and I love holding you . . ."

"Wouldn't you know if you're gay?" Anna interrupted. "Maybe you're bisexual. Everybody who's getting married is promising to be faithful even though they know they'll be attracted to other people. When you get married, you'll just be promising to be faithful to me even though you know you'll sometimes be attracted to other women and maybe other men, too."

"The problem is that I'm worrying so much about being gay. I don't know if these thoughts will ever stop. I'm afraid they won't stop. They'll keep growing."

Anna thought about this while Carlos drained the last of his cold coffee. "You know," she decided, "I think you should talk to someone who knows more about this than I do."

CARLOS IN MY OFFICE

He was so nervous he could hardly sit down. I introduced myself, offered him water, and decided not to offer him coffee. He was too wired already.

"There's a movie going in my head," he told me. "It's got men having sex with men, and I can't make the movie stop."

"That sounds really difficult," I said.

"And people look at me all the time, and I can tell they think I'm gay. That's what they whisper behind my back. There's a guy on my shift. He says I act gay, and I can't tell if he's kidding or not. He says when I look at men, I look too long. That means I'm gay."

"Did you tell him you aren't gay, and you want him to stop hassling you about it?"

"Yeah, but now it's a big joke. He won't let it go. He likes that it bothers me."

Carlos was a very good-looking man in his late twenties. He had had men approach him and flirt with him sexually—even ask him to have sexual hookups. The first time it didn't bother him, but when it happened several more times, he became concerned that they saw something in him that he couldn't see in himself. He was terrified that these guys could see that he was gay, and that's why they were coming on to him.

"I stopped shopping at the mall," Carlos told me. "Everybody looks at me. They think I'm gay."

I went though my evaluation with him over several sessions, but he didn't seem to be at all gay. Basically, he wasn't turned on by guys. Even though he worried about being gay, he was free of the homophobia typical of closeted gays who don't know they're gay. Some might say he was homophobic, because he worried about being gay. Their thinking might go, "If he's worried about it, then he must think something is wrong with it." But his issue wasn't about being gay. It was about the anxiety generated in his crazy-making circular thinking: knowing he isn't gay but fearing he is, but knowing he isn't but fearing he is . . .

I asked Carlos to tell me about his childhood, what it was like in his family when he was growing up. It turns out his obsessing began when he was thirteen. He went through some other obsessions—fear of committing suicide, fear that masturbation would lead to infertility, and others. Then, his worries about being gay started.

"It's funny how this happened," he told me. "I started thinking about what I could do that would make my father the most angry at me, and it just popped into my head, 'He'd kill me if I were gay.' Then I started worrying about it, and I couldn't stop worrying about it."

Carlos's only same-sex experience happened before he was ten years old, some looking and touching with another boy. He admitted, "When I'm not worrying about it, my fantasies are about women, but when I get anxious, I hit the gay porn sites to see if they turn me on." He told me he found them a bit interesting, but he'd never been sexually aroused by them. He'd never been sexually aroused by a man either.

Carlos told me he was one of four boys in a family in which his father was a well-respected member of a very small, very rural, very Catholic community. "Being homosexual was akin to Satanism," he said. "Right was right, wrong was wrong, and there was no in-between, not even a little bit." He didn't remember any sexual abuse or "excessive" corporal punishment or family violence. Still, I found it very significant that all three of his siblings were being medicated for anxiety disorders. In fact, Carlos had previously been treated with medication for anxiety, although that had been years before.

"I've thought maybe I should get a male escort to try things with," he admitted. "I got some contact information online. Maybe that would get me past this thing. Right now, every male I see, I wonder, 'Do I find him attractive?' and 'Would I want to have sex with him?' and like that, all the time. I can't stop these thoughts.

"But Anna . . . ," he said. It was almost a cry. "I'm so lucky to have found Anna. She loves me. She's wonderful. How can I be messing up everything with Anna this way?"

"Are you planning to get married?"

"Yes. I asked her, and she said yes. Her family loves me. My mother loves her. My father hasn't objected. My brothers say she's too good for me, and I agree. She's the best thing that has ever happened to me, but look at what I'm doing. I'm messing up everything. What's going on? Why do I act this way? Can't I just stop worrying about it? I'm not gay. I want Anna. Help me stop this movie that keeps running in my head."

HOMOSEXUAL OBSESSIVE COMPULSIVE DISORDER

Perhaps the most extreme form of anxiety over gay identity is Homosexual Obsessive Compulsive Disorder (HOCD). Although HOCD is not an official diagnosis sanctioned by the American Psychological Association, those suffering from it have taken it upon themselves to label and address it.[2]

> *Homosexual Obsessive Compulsive Disorder*—HOCD is exemplified by a man worrying about being gay so constantly and compulsively that it takes up a good deal of his life and causes him significant anxiety.

A man with HOCD is preoccupied with the idea that he might be gay. His behavior is fixated and uncontrollable the way someone with OCD can be obsessed with cleanliness, washing his hands hundreds of times a day; checking so many times to see if he's turned off the stove that he can't leave home; or hoarding enormous collections of worthless items.

The HOCD man will obsess about being gay to the point that he believes he *is* gay. He might decide to try sex with men, which typically leaves him feeling unsatisfied and uncomfortable. These bad feelings make sense, because he isn't gay but rather is acting under the influence of his anxiety-driven compulsion.

The following list of characteristics of HOCD is adapted from brainphysics.com. A person has HOCD if he or she

- has worries or intrusive thoughts about being homosexual,
- feels an inability to get rid of these worries or intrusive thoughts,
- sees a person of the same gender and immediately feels anxiety about being a homosexual,
- avoids people of the same gender from fear of being attracted to them,
- worries about giving off signals that he or she may be homosexual,
- repeats mundane actions for fear that these actions may have been performed in a "homosexual" way or a way that may signal homosexuality. For example, a male may feel the need to get up from a chair and sit back down if he feels that the way he sat before was "feminine," or a male may worry that the way he walks is too "feminine" or signals homosexuality.

Monnica Williams warns that mental health professionals may misdiagnose a man with HOCD as a gay man coming out.[3] Many of the characteristics in this list might be shared by a gay man desperate to believe he's straight. He would, for example, be repulsed by his own gay thoughts. For HOCD Carlos, the gay thoughts are unwanted because they're not who he is. For the gay guy in the closet, they're unwanted because they're not who he wants to be.

Even though a diagnostician may be confused by HOCD, the difference is easy to test. A straight man with HOCD will not test gay using the list at the end of chapter 1. Note that the HOCD guy is not homophobic, which is item 7 on the list. He will say, "If I'm gay, okay, but I don't feel gay." The closeted gay man will tend to be much more antagonistic toward gays and "the gay lifestyle."

WHAT CARLOS AND ANNA DECIDE TO DO

Over several sessions, I convinced Carlos that he wasn't gay, and then we worked on his OCD. Medications had helped him before, so I arranged for him to see a psychiatrist who could prescribe for him while we continued his psychotherapy.

Carlos and Anna came to see me together for one session. She was an assistant manager of a beauty salon. She was used to making things happen and was not about to let Carlos's worries disable their future together. She urged him to follow his heart and give his head a rest.

"I'm scared," Carlos told Anna and me. "I'm scared that in the future I might feel bad about whatever decisions we make now."

By this, I took him to mean his marriage to Anna. He had told me in a previous session that she was remarkably patient and loving with him, but now, in my office, she seemed impatient.

"When you talk about being scared that way," she told him, "you scare me. I think you're going to disappear on me. It makes me feel unsafe with you, and I've never ever felt unsafe with you."

Carlos didn't respond at first. His face sagged. He looked very sad, and maybe a little hurt. "I'm sorry," he said in a small voice. He seemed to struggle to say more, but nothing came out.

Then, Anna did something remarkable. She got up from her chair, went to kneel by his chair, and took his hand. "Look at me," she said, because he had been looking at the floor. "I love you," she said, "and I fully accept who you are, with all your fears and worries." She smiled, and he allowed himself a little echo smile. "We know that if we get married, life will not always be easy. It isn't always easy for anyone." Carlos nodded. It was a gesture of acquiescence. "I hear that you're afraid," she went on, not giving him a chance to start his extended ruminations again. "So, here's your choice: You can be scared and alone. Or scared and with me."

Carlos certainly looked scared, but his eyes held a glimmer of hope. Anna wasn't finished.

"Can we set a date for our marriage?" she asked. "Be with me for the next fifty years? You have to decide now, here, in Dr. Kort's office. Are we leaving here as a couple, or separately—and part ways forever?"

"I could never walk away from you," Carlos said. "You are my soul mate."

She smiled more fully now. A hint of gentle mockery was in her tone. "Is that a *yes*, Carlos?"

"Yes," he agreed. He took both of her hands in his. "Yes, yes, yes. If you'll take me with all that's wrong with me. . . . I can hardly believe you love me that much."

"Carlos," I said quietly, and they both turned to look at me. "You've made great progress. The medications are helping, and I think you're just about through with your therapy. You can let this go. You don't have to worry anymore."

A few months later they let me know they had married.

DON'T WORRY, BE HAPPY

The core of Carlos's anxiety was society's homophobia. His strict upbringing may have added fire to the flames of this common prejudice. His body chemistry may have made him particularly susceptible to OCD. Luckily, he responded to standard treatments for OCD, medication and therapy. It certainly helped that he had found such a supportive and forceful woman who wanted to share his life.

* * *

In the next chapter, Sam feels the strong pull of his bisexuality, but Jillian doesn't think she can tolerate what he proposes. As always, how they choose to resolve the conflict is a very personal decision that nobody else can make for them.

7

SAM WON'T CHEAT ON JILLIAN

What Are the Bisexual Options?

Yes, I Really Am Bisexual. Deal with It.

—Wilson Diehl [1]

Sam came to consult with me. He was depressed and desperate. He was even talking about suicide.

"If I'd been smart enough to try this out when I was in college, maybe it wouldn't be such a big deal now," he told me. He loved his wife, Jillian. He was turned on by her. They had great sex. But he felt that he needed to have sex with a man. He couldn't explain it, but it seemed very important.

"Let's try to find out what's going on," I told him.

I saw him for several months before concluding that he was bisexual. What made his case a little tricky to sort out was that he had never had any sexual experiences with men, only women. I had to rule out childhood abuse and other issues that might lead a straight man to feel he needed to have sex with men. But Sam didn't feel compelled. He wasn't curious. He wasn't responding to a whim. He was truly sexually turned on by men as well as women.

"I need to do this," he told me more than once, *this* being to find a man he trusted and liked for some sexual encounters. He didn't want to go behind Jillian's back. I commended him on his commitment to her, and I told him he'd better start talking about this with her.

The next session Sam told me he had tried to talk with Jillian, but he said she "felt threatened" and got mad, and he couldn't stand upsetting her. So, they could hardly talk. At Sam's request, they came to see me together.

* * *

"Why did you lie to me?" was practically the first thing she said to him in my office. She turned to me. "Is he gay and doesn't know it?"

I explained to her about bisexuality. Some gay men appear to be bisexual as they are first coming out, but I've had enough experience with gay men coming out to be able to tell the difference. After the months of work Sam and I had done together, I felt certain of my evaluation. She didn't seem to feel comforted.

"I don't trust you," she said to him.

"I'll just forget about it," Sam said. "It's okay. I'll just push it away. I won't act on it."

Jillian made a dismissive gesture with her hand. "I don't know how you're going to be able to do that."

"I will. I don't want this to separate us."

"How will I know?"

"I've always been honest with you."

"You didn't tell me you've been thinking about this ever since we got married. For eight years, and you never told me. What else haven't you told me?"

"I told you before we got married."

"You said it was just some fantasies. That it wasn't a problem. Now you tell me you have to go find a man. And what? Be unfaithful? Decide you're gay? Leave me?"

"I'm not being unfaithful. I'm talking to you. I want to be honest. It's just something I have to do. I don't want to leave you."

"How can I believe anything you say?"

"I've never lied to you."

"I can't trust you about anything. Maybe you haven't technically lied, but you sure didn't tell me what you were cooking up behind my back."

Sam looked distraught. He turned to me. "Maybe you can help me put this away. Help me just forget about it."

Jillian's distress was hard for him to take.

"Here's the thing," I said. "Of course, you have choices in how you behave. You've chosen to come here with Jillian and talk to me. You didn't have to do that. It was a choice. You chose to tell Jillian what you're dealing with.

"Some things you can choose, but you can't choose your nature. You can't choose your sexual identity. You can't choose not to be bisexual."

"So, does this mean he has to have sex with men?" she asked me.

"What he needs to do is not for me to say," I told her. "What do you think, Sam?"

"I feel like I really need to have relations with men," he said. "If I don't do this, I'm going to go crazy. I feel so depressed. But I realize if Jillian thinks I'm being unfaithful, then I could lose her, and that's depressing, too, so I'm in this horrible situation."

"Even if you're being perfectly honest right now," Jillian said, "and I say, 'Okay, do what you have to do,' maybe you'll end up deciding you're gay. What about that? Aren't you worried you won't want to be with me anymore?"

Sam turned to me with such a pleading look that I decided I should say something. "Sam is bisexual. That much we've established in his therapy. Is he likely to go off and be trapped by his 'gay side' and never return to you? That seems unlikely to me and to him." Sam was nodding agreement. "However," I went on, "any couple has to work to stay together in a healthy and happy way."

Sam loved Jillian and he loved being married to her. They had talked about having children. He wanted her to see that he wasn't just an adulterer with sophisticated excuses; he was a man of integrity who had to acknowledge his identity. He wanted her support, and she was understandably feeling very challenged. "Isn't what Sam wants really some kind of open marriage?" she asked. "What kind of wife would allow her man that?"

"Sam is presenting you with a lot to process," I said to her. "I think you need to be in your own therapy, either with me or your own private therapist. You shouldn't have to work all this out right now without time to feel what you're feeling and talk about what this is bringing up for you. And you definitely need to work on this without having to worry about Sam's reactions for a while."

Jillian decided to take my advice, and she found herself a therapist.

SEX ON THE SIDE

What's the difference between a straight man acting on a trauma-induced compulsion to have sex with men and a bisexual whose identity requires acknowledgment? And, for that matter, a simple philanderer? To an outside superficial observer, their behaviors may look the same, but—and this is the core of the insight needed to understand what's happening here—*the roots of the behavior and its drivers are different.* Sam's need was all the more compelling, because he'd never explored his sexuality by having relations with men.

A bisexual guy might not need to have relations with both genders for his whole life. I've treated other bisexuals who've explored both sides of their sexuality before they got married and that was enough. "Yep. I'm bisexual. Those were great times. Loved it. I don't need to do it anymore." Other bisexuals find they want to have relations with both genders all their lives. Sam felt he needed to have sex with men especially because he had never done it, and he honestly didn't know if it would be a lifetime thing.

A period of exploration for gay men before they settle down, the so-called gay adolescence, is well recognized. Less discussed is this "bisexual adolescence," but the same developmental process seems to be operating.

My bisexual friends and associates want me to make sure to say here that many bisexuals can make a choice to be monogamous. Like anybody else, personal factors for bisexuals are part of the equation in how people manage their life choices. Bisexuals can choose to be monogamous, but Sam seemed to need at least a period of sexual exploration.

JILLIAN'S SIDE OF THE STORY

It didn't take Jillian long to bring back the fruits of her therapy for the three of us to consider.

"My mother would scream at my father, literally scream at him, all the time about him having affairs," she told us. "If he worked late, if he went on a business trip. . . . He traveled on business a lot. He was a manufacturing engineer at Ford. They sent him to plants to help them get past problems. If they wanted him, he had to drop everything and go. Time was always of the essence."

"Was your father having affairs?" I asked her.

Jillian paused. "I don't know. He always denied it. Mother never caught him red-handed or anything. But she made me feel like he was keeping secrets and lying, and her rage fairly dripped from the ceiling of our house every day. I hated it."

"So," I said, "it's bad enough to have your husband tell you he's bisexual and wants sex with men, but now you're telling us you have a history with your mother raging at your father about extramarital sex. It's a double whammy. I can see why you can barely tolerate what Sam is suggesting. It feels exactly like what your mother feared your dad was doing."

"I guess that's right," Jillian agreed. "It was such a relief to get out of my parents' house, get away from her screaming, get away from her anger, get away from secrets and lying. I don't ever want to experience anything like that again. I don't want to have to deal with what she dealt with. I don't want to become her."

"That makes perfect sense to me," I told her. "I imagine most women would feel the way you do, even without your mother's worries about affairs. Still, your situation with Sam is different, because your father denied everything, and Sam is being up front about what he wants."

Jillian nodded. "I know. I guess I see that he has to do this, but I can't be under the same roof with him when he does it." She turned to Sam. "We need to separate. Go do what you need to do and then come back to me when it's over. I can't take living with an unfaithful husband."

Sam was silent.

"You can see what she's dealing with," I said to him.

"Anyway," she told us, "I just don't want to see it happening."

I spent some of Sam's individual therapy sessions going over with him how Jillian was having to face a bad situation on top of a bad situation: her sense of betrayal that he would want sex with someone else and the effect on her of her childhood trauma, her mother's fear of affairs, screaming at her father. I wanted him to understand why it was so difficult for her to give him the "go-ahead," and he totally understood. At the same time, he had his own set of special issues.

SAM'S SIDE OF THE STORY

Sam's father had been in the U.S. Air Force through a good deal of Sam's childhood. That left their mother pretty much to raise him and his brothers.

She was overwhelmed and overworked, and Sam spent his childhood anxious to placate her. She would explode when things weren't going well, and he tried hard never to upset her. He decided as a boy to do everything she wanted.

As an adult, Sam was not very good at negotiating with his wife. At the slightest sign that she was upset, he was in a panic to appease her just as young Sam had been in a panic to appease his mother. Now, he was caught between his powerful need to express his bisexuality and his powerful need to placate the woman he lived with.

COMPROMISES

We had been working together for three months when Sam came to a decision. He said to Jillian, "I'm ready to try that separation," meaning the separation she had set as a condition for him to experiment. "I don't love the idea," he said, "but if that's the only way . . ."

Jillian started to cry. The hurt on her face as she looked at her husband was naked and extreme. Then, suddenly, her mood switched to outrage. "How can you do this to me?" she screamed at him. Sam's eyes went wide with shock. I could imagine how Jillian's response was affecting a mother pleaser like Sam, even as I sympathized with Jillian.

"This has to be really hard for you," I said to her. "I understand that." I turned to Sam. "And this must be equally hard for you, because I know how much you want to please Jillian. Part of that comes from your childhood, trying to please your mother."

Jillian seemed to catch herself. She stopped screaming, and a long moment of silence filled the room. Then she said, "I guess I'm acting like my mother. I'm having my own childhood response." She stood up and went to sit by Sam on the couch. "You are not going to leave me," she said. She had tears in her eyes, and so did Sam. Finally, I intervened.

"So, what I hear you saying," I said to her, "is that separation isn't going to work for you when before you thought it would."

She nodded. "I thought it would be okay, but I've changed my mind. I don't want to live without him."

Fair enough, but they still needed to work out something.

* * *

They were having good sex all during this time. In fact, Jillian was encouraging a more active sex life than they had had before. Sometimes, when a woman fears that her husband is wanting sex out of the house, she thinks: *If I give him more sex, then he won't want sex with someone else.* However, Sam's need wasn't about that. He said to her in my office when I raised the issue, "I love the quality and the quantity of our sex and I always have. I'm not unhappy in any way about it."

"Well, why do you want men?" she asked.

He replied, "My need for men has nothing to do with you."

* * *

The next idea they came up with was remarkably creative, and a first in my practice. They agreed that if he had to find men for sex, then they'd do it as a threesome. They'd do it together. She took charge of the whole thing. The plan was to meet a bi man, so there wouldn't be a threat that a gay man would want to take Sam away from her. She went online to see who she could find. Of course, there were guys who wanted to do threesomes. There always are. But typically, they are more into the wife than the husband. This is the setup: The prize is the woman, but you have to have sex with the guy, too. Lots of men are into that. Cuckolding, as described in chapter 3, is one variation. Jillian set up an anonymous e-mail with the title: "We're a married couple, looking for a third." This quickly got many responses, and Sam and Jillian met several of the men, none of whom they liked. Finally, after a month they met a man who seemed reasonable. They both liked him. He was bi. He wanted to help them as well as himself.

Then, suddenly, but maybe predictably, Jillian backed out, and she was angry. She went back to, "How could you do this to me?" and Sam went back to being devastated to have caused her such grief.

* * *

We regrouped. Sam was nervous but persistent. "I have these needs, but I want to stay married to you."

So now she said, "I guess you're going to have to do it. You're going to have to do it without me, but I don't want you to leave. I don't want to separate. Let's stay a couple, but I do want to meet the guy you're going to do it with when you find him. I want to meet him for coffee, I want to know a little bit about him, but I don't want to have sex with him."

Sam was okay with this. He was nothing if not a compromiser.

"I don't think I could watch you enjoying a guy," she added.

So that was the new plan. She didn't want to be involved sexually, but she wanted to meet the man and know him and then let her husband have sex with him.

WHAT IS A BISEXUAL?

We have used "the beach test" and "youthful noticing" as indicators of a person's tendency to be straight or gay. The spirit of these tests is that a man's sexual identity is closely linked to the responses of his vision system. What gender he responds to on the beach (or elsewhere, of course, but the response is more primal if the people are nearly naked) strongly indicates his identity. Again, the spirit here is a response before the "thinking" part of the brain has a chance to process, filter, and impose moral rules on the response. (Women's sexuality seems to be wired in a more fluid and less visual way and is not a part of our discussion.)[2] In the beach test, we expect a bisexual man to be attracted to both genders, although scientific research on the sexual desire of bisexuals is complicated by various issues, such as the exact definition of a bisexual.[3]

What's the difference between sexual desire and sexual identity? When Sam said he "had" to try out having sex with men, what did he mean? Sam was a very honest guy, so it's clear he didn't just mean he had a whim or a desire for a good time. He held his desire to have sex with men as a "need." What's happening here?

When we use the term "identity," we are trying to capture something about a person's core. We understand that sometimes people need to claim their core, to proclaim allegiance to the tribe of people like them. Suppressing this need can lead to depression, hopelessness, and even suicide. The *sexual* needs of bisexuals vary greatly, depending on other aspects of their situations, but the need to claim a bisexual identity is common to all.

When people "self-identify" their sexual identity, we have to be careful that two conditions are satisfied: (1) the people know what they're talking about, and (2) they're being honest. Assuming these conditions, we tend to "take a person's word for it" when he or she identifies as gay, straight, or bi.

I feel the need to emphasize that bisexual and gay identities are distinct and different. A person is not bisexual for a while and then turns gay. Gay men coming out may believe (or claim) for a time that they are bisexual, especially if they are in love with a woman or have had sex with women. The truth is that if a man "ends up" gay, he was gay all along.

I have had a lot of experience counseling men coming out gay, as well as coming out bi, and in therapy any ambiguity eventually clarifies itself. Admittedly, it is challenging to arrive at a correct diagnosis at the time of maximum confusion, anxiety, and dread that may be a part of the coming-out process. That a gay man might fall in love with a woman while not desiring women in general may seem unbelievable, but I've seen it many times. Having sex with men doesn't make a man gay; having sex with women doesn't make him straight or bi.

Bisexuality is complex. Whole books have been written devoted merely to understanding what bisexuality is—for example, Fritz Klein's pioneering *The Bisexual Option*,[4] published in 1978. This book presents a systematic argument that bisexuality is a real sexual orientation and should be taken seriously by the psychotherapeutic community. A more recent treatment of the topic is given in *Dual Attraction: Understanding Bisexuality*.[5] Benedict Cary wrote an article in 2005, "Straight, Gay, or Lying? Bisexuality Revisited," summarizing some of the persistent controversies.[6] A more "bisexual friendly" summary is given in "The Scientific Quest to Prove—Once and For All—That Someone Can Be Truly Attracted to Both a Man and a Woman: Bisexuality Comes Out of the Closet."[7] The website bisexual.org is a good place to get other people's stories and current thoughts about bisexuality.

THERE ISN'T ANY ONE "BISEXUAL STORY"

I'll tell you how the story of Sam and Jillian worked out, but first I want to make sure I am clear on one thing. Their story isn't "typical" of all bisexuals. It's just one way things can go.

For Sam and Jillian, bisexuality was not even their primary problem. The other issues in their relationship needed to be addressed so that they could have a more successful marriage: Sam was a people pleaser, and that got in the way of his ability to negotiate with Jillian for what he needed. He had to learn to be more straightforward and less fearful. Jillian had unresolved issues that had resulted from her mom accusing her dad of affairs. Jillian had to get past the raging that had been programmed into her in her childhood. She had to learn to express her concerns in ways that her partner could hear. Sam and Jillian's encounter over bisexuality became an opportunity for their marriage to grow. (This is an illustration of the Imago process for couples therapy, where a person's conflicts with his or her partner's issues are taken as opportunities for growth. See chapter 15.)

Sam was allowed to look for a man to have sex with; the agreement was that he would keep Jillian informed and at least offer her the opportunity to meet the man before Sam had sex with him. Neither of them wanted Sam to be involved with anonymous one-night stands. Sam needed to feel connected to the man, so Jillian's condition wasn't a problem for him.

He learned to use Grindr and other "gay finding apps." He used Craigslist. He met a lot of men for coffee, just as someone dating would, although he refused to call what he was doing "dating," because romance wasn't on the table. On the other hand, he was bi, and he wanted at least some thrill of gay sexual excitement. He found a few men. Jillian did have coffee with one. Then she told Sam she trusted him, and she'd rather not know any more.

Sam was naturally faithful and naturally monogamous, but he needed to confirm and explore his bisexuality. In his case, he needed only a year of sex outside marriage.

It's not that Sam wasn't really bi, or that all bi men need just a year of sex with men. Sam was bi, is bi, and will always be bi. It is a core part of his identity. However, having a relatively brief period for "identity confirmation" was enough for him.

* * *

In the next chapter, we meet a gay husband who is coming out. He has lived in a heterosexual marriage for ten years and loves his wife and children. Now he is tormented by his need to express his identity. What are his, and their, realistic options after building a whole life together?

8

DOES JACOB HAVE TO LEAVE KATELYN?

The Gay Husband

He sat down on the bed and said, "I have something I need to tell you." He took a deep breath. "I'm homosexual."

—Jane Isay[1]

Katelyn and Jacob sat in my office. He held in his arms his sleeping six-month-old baby girl, incongruously small against the large man's chest. While the baby slept in the serenity of total trust, her father's tears fell around her like bombs.

Of course, tears have fallen before in my office. That's what the strategically placed boxes of tissues are for. But it was the first time in the months I'd been seeing Jacob that his impossible situation had spilled over in this way.

"I can't do it," he was saying. He was looking at Katelyn, and her eyes were beginning to get moist, too. "I told you that if we had another child, I would find a way to commit to our marriage, but I just can't do it. I tried. I really tried. We've been together for ten years. I love you. I love our children, my little girls." He looked down at the baby in his arms, who still wasn't stirring.

"You can't leave now," Katelyn said. "We've made such progress. I've forgiven you. Why can't you forgive yourself?"

Jacob was wiping ineffectively at his eyes with one hand while balancing the baby in the other. His nose was running. I got up and put a tissue in his hand.

"Everything between us was fine," Katelyn persisted. "You just had some stupid affairs. I've forgiven you."

"No," Jacob yelled, and now the baby did open her eyes. "Don't you understand? I'm gay. I met guys. I had to meet them. I avoided it as long as I could. I knew I was kinky when I married you, but I didn't know I was gay."

"Other men can have self-control," Katelyn said, a little edge cutting her sympathy. I noticed her tears had stopped.

The baby began to cry along with her father.

WHY ISN'T EVERYTHING PERFECT?

Jacob had married his middle-school girlfriend, the only girlfriend he had ever had. He really did love her, but when your identity comes calling, you can't refuse to open the door. Jacob should have known he was gay from the moment his preadolescent "noticing" of boys eclipsed any interest he might have had in girls. But he simply could not recognize the signs in himself, because he had learned from an early age that he shouldn't be, couldn't be, gay. He latched onto Katelyn in the eighth grade.

He wanted a girlfriend. She wanted a boyfriend. She was affectionate and kindhearted. He was affectionate and kindhearted. They were easy company for each other. They even liked the same movies.

Toy Story was their favorite, even though it was for little kids, and they were fifteen when it came out. They saw it together a dozen times. And *Babe*. And *Clueless*. *Twelve Monkeys* was a rare disagreement between them. He understood being totally alien in your own country. She thought it was stupid and scary.

They did their homework together, made nighttime runs to McDonalds, and held hands at high school football games. Long before graduation, their parents had accepted that they would get married. Although they had agreed they'd be reasonable and finish community college before they tied the knot, they had great and frequent sex, and when Katelyn got pregnant during her junior year in college, they and their families took it in stride. They immediately got married, baby Sally was born, and that was that.

They lived with her parents until Jacob graduated, and Katelyn wasn't too upset to have to go to college part time with both sets of grandparents to help with the babysitting and the bills. They got their own home when Jacob found his first real job, a sales rep for a big heating-and-cooling firm. He sold giant air-conditioning units, the kind that are installed by helicopter on the top of factories. He was friendly and earnest. He was smart and easily picked up the technical lingo he needed to explain the benefits of his company's products. People trusted his low-key persuasion, and he did well as a salesman. After she graduated, Katelyn found work as a part-time bank teller, and she thought she could be a branch manager one day when she could work full time.

But, of course, all was not right in Jacob and Katelyn's marriage from the beginning. Jacob's self-proclaimed "kinkiness" included a fascination with gay porn, which he didn't share with Katelyn. The Internet was a cornucopia of possibilities. He began to read Craigslist and looked for straight guys who wanted to hook up just to "try it out." He resisted meeting anyone for the first five years of their marriage, but by the time he was twenty-five the attraction was overwhelming, and he began to arrange meetings. But he had rules. Never the same guy twice. That would be "too gay." And never anywhere sleazy. It had to be at someone's home or at least a hotel.

Despite his conflicts and guilt, he loved everything about sex with guys: hugging, spooning, kissing, sucking, fucking. By the rules, when it was over, it was over: no dinner, no names, never meet again. Call it a "hookup," never a "date." Like a bomb dropped in the ocean, the waters quickly covered over the explosive possibilities of a real relationship with a man, and after every encounter Jacob could believe that maybe he had "gotten it out of his system" at last, and he'd never need to do it again.

A month would pass, and then he did it all over again with someone else. And he had no idea at all, zero, that he might be gay. He looked at gay men, and he didn't see himself in them at all. "I'm just a little out-of-the-box" was what he told himself. "I'm just curious about stuff." And he believed that that was all there was to it.

Meanwhile, he and Katelyn were having the silliest, stupidest arguments. Not about sex. They had frequent good sex.

"Why do you need so many shoes?" Jacob asked her on more than one occasion, and so they would argue about money.

"Why do you need to bring the baby into our bed?" This really did irritate him. "I have to go sleep on the couch."

"You don't have to sleep on the couch."

"Well, I do too have to sleep on the couch. I need my sleep so I can pay your bills."

"You're so unreasonable."

"You're so stubborn."

They would always make up quickly. Neither could hold a grudge for more than twenty-four hours. Neither could live without the affirming touch of the other.

"I'm sorry. It was my fault."

"I lost my temper. It was my fault. I know you love me."

"I do love you so much."

And so like a typical young couple, they lived a normal life of establishing themselves: with each other, as parents, in their jobs, in their social life. Katelyn didn't begin her work at the bank until Sally could go to preschool.

But over the years Jacob was gone more, out later, missed more suppers, and their arguments took on a edge of underlying distrust. Katelyn "jokingly" asked him if he was having affairs and then was horrified by his pause, his blushes, before he denied it. The fights got nastier, and they were about even more trivial things.

"Who forgot to load the dishwasher?"

"Why are you hogging the remote?"

Now one or the other would leave the room angry or crying, or both, and making up wasn't as easy as it had been when they were first married.

Just as the worst of her morning sickness was abating in her second pregnancy, she discovered on Jacob's computer the history of his gay porn viewing. Hundreds of sites. She'd never seen anything like it. Still, she didn't tell him what she'd found. She just started questioning him.

"Are you gay?" she asked.

"No. Of course not."

"Are you sure? I'm starting to wonder."

"Why are you wondering?"

"I don't know. I'm just wondering."

Then she told him she had found his porn. He still wouldn't admit anything.

"That was just a pop-up," he said. "I closed it as soon as it opened. You know those porn sites do that."

"But in your history, hundreds . . ."

"I'm not . . . What you found . . . It's just fun fetish stuff. It doesn't mean a thing."

And the next week, she'd raise the topic again. She couldn't let it go. "Wait a minute, you told me *no*, but . . . why did you go to those sites? And you went to a chat room. I saw it, and why would you be doing that?"

"I told you, they're just pop-ups. You go to one site, it takes you to another." Now he was actively lying, covering his tracks.

It went on for months: *Are you? Are you? Are you? No. No. No.*

After the new baby came, he changed his story. "Yes, I did look at those sites. Yes, I did some chatting, but I've never met anyone. I know I'm kinky, but that's all."

"Well," she pushed, "if you've never met anyone, how do you know you're not gay? Maybe you *are* gay."

"Well, I don't know how I know. I just know. Can't I just know? We straight people know we're straight."

Finally, after months of this and taking care of the new baby, as well as a nine-year-old, they were both exhausted, and he saw that the baby made no difference in the core of his feelings about men, so finally he admitted it. "Okay, yes. I've slept with a few guys. It doesn't mean anything. No way I'm gay."

He went on. "Even if I could be gay, I'm never going to leave you. I love you. This is the family I want."

At this time, it was hard for Jacob to imagine losing his family and his place in the community. He really did love being with Katelyn, and he loved his kids. He liked having a "normal" family, and he didn't want to lose it.

Then he realized he wasn't feeling sexual anymore toward Katelyn. He could no longer keep his erections when he was with her, a problem he'd never had in the past. His panic at his erectile dysfunction, and not the possibility that he might be gay, motivated him to seek me, a sexologist, for advice.

JACOB GETS IT

But pretty soon Jacob told me he was having affairs with men, and it was natural to ask him if he thought he might be gay. He strongly resisted the idea.

"Even if I were gay," he told me, "I couldn't live that way. Those gay guys lead superficial lives. They have hundreds of sex partners. They don't value family or relationships. It's just sex, sex, sex. They get AIDS. That's not me. Not that I'm prejudiced about homosexuals. It's just no way me."

"What you're describing," I replied, "is pure homophobia. It's not true, but I do often hear this kind of negativity about gay culture . . . from gay men who are hiding their gayness from themselves."

He looked sheepish, like maybe he was dimly aware he was protesting too much. "I thought maybe if Katelyn and I had another child," he said, "I could get all this behind me."

"You mean the way you've been seeking sex with men?"

"Yeah, and the porn. I just can't stay away from the porn. Maybe my problem is I'm a sex addict—porn, sex with men. It fits doesn't it?"

"It could fit," I agreed, "but when a man is suppressing his homosexuality, his identity often expresses itself as compulsive sexual behavior."

"When baby Sally came," Jacob said, "we were busy, and I didn't have time for anything but school, my job, and the baby. I thought maybe, if we had another child, I wouldn't have time for porn or anything."

"How did that work out?"

"We had Megan just last January. It didn't help at all. I still can't stop seeing men."

"When as a child did you first start noticing boys?" I asked him, as gently as I could. And so we went through it all, including the list at the end of chapter 1: youthful noticing, the beach test. He'd already shown me his homophobia. I let it unfold over a few sessions, but it wasn't really difficult to figure out. He realized it himself. A lightbulb went on. His denial evaporated.

"I'm a gay man?" he said to me one day, shoulders slumping with defeat.

"You're a gay man," I agreed. "And now you have to decide what you're going to choose to do with the rest of your life. You have options.

You and Katelyn have options. Don't you think it's time the three of us got together?"

JACOB AND KATELYN, CONTINUED

The baby was still crying, but Jacob had stopped.

"I thought you told me you were going to try to make this work," Katelyn said to him. "You said you could make it work."

Jacob was looking at the floor, miserable and guilty. "I thought I could make it work," he said, "but the more I've talked about it, the more I've explored it, I can't fight it."

"Can't you just look at porn?" Katelyn offered. "Can't you just have your fantasies? I'll let you have all the stupid porn you want. Why do you have to do this to us? Destroy our family after ten years together? Just so you can lead some gay lifestyle. Do you really think that's going to work for you?"

"You know I love you," Jacob said. "I don't want to hurt you. I càn't help it."

"You lied to me," Katelyn countered. "You're lying to me now, so you can't love me. You betrayed me. You cheated on me with those men."

"It wasn't like that," Jacob said, but Katelyn was no longer in the mood for bargains.

She stood and snatched little Megan from Jacob's arms. "I'm going to make it so you will never see this baby again." As she exited, she threw over her shoulder, "And you'll never see Sally again either."

Jacob stared in shock at my office door left gaping open. He turned to me. "I thought she'd understand," he said. "We love each other."

MONTHS OF SHOCK

Despite the big blowup in my office, Jacob and Katelyn continued to see me for couples counseling. She quickly got her own therapist, as I recommended, and was doing her own individual therapy at the same time. She was deep into her pain. She told Jacob things like: "You've hurt me. How could you do this to our family? You never loved me. You just wanted children. Now what about me? You ruined my life. I'm never going to recover. Who's going to want me now? I'm going to be almost thirty-five with two little children."

But at other times she told him: "I love you. I don't want you to go. We can try to make this work. Maybe you're bi. You've been having sex with me. You must be bi. How could you not be bi and have sex with a woman?"

But the betrayal loomed large for her, and her pain was sometimes overwhelming. "Our whole marriage has been a sham. You never loved me. You've lied to me all along. You just wanted me so you could pass as normal."

"Why are you being so nasty and vindictive?" a bewildered Jacob asked his wife in more than one session. "I don't get it."

"After all your lies and cheating," she told him, "what did you expect?"

Soon she started telling their extended families that Jacob was gay, wanting him to feel the shame she was feeling. She and Jacob agreed they wouldn't tell Sally, but Katelyn told her anyway. When a mixed-orientation couple is separating, I often recommend they not talk to the children about "gay," just talk about "divorce." Gay can come later, but divorce and gay at the same time is a lot for a child to have to hear. Katelyn agreed in my office, but she was angry and wanted him to suffer just like she was suffering. And telling Sally was another way she could hurt him and let him know how badly he'd screwed up.

I referred her to the Straight Spouse Network.[2] At first, she found it reassuring to understand that her situation wasn't unique and that giving evasive answers and denials was common for gay husbands confused and coming out. She heard stories of couples who had reached accommodation of the husband's gayness or bi-ness, as well as many angry stories from disappointed wives of gay husbands. However, the sheer volume and variety of the stories left her confused and did nothing to calm her anger.

Of course she was angry. It's so normal. Who wouldn't be? And sad, and feeling betrayed. She couldn't get over his deception. "You lied to me," she said to him, over and over.

But it's so much more complicated than that. Gays and lesbians are rewarded for building a life around lies. Imagine you're a gay little boy. You're told you're not really gay. You're not supposed to be gay. Straight is the direction you have to go. Any good little boy will say, "No problem. I'd rather go that route anyway." Jacob had no permission as he was growing up to explore anything in his sexuality that wasn't straight. Jacob didn't merely lie to his wife. He was lied to, which made him lie to himself, which then, in turn, caused him to build his life around lies.

In my office for an individual session, Jacob was feeling horribly guilty. He'd told Katelyn he'd use her divorce lawyer, and she could have anything she wanted.

I told him, "You're going to regret that later. You feel shame and guilt, but you're not her perpetrator. I know she told you, 'This is all your fault. You should have known better.' You're certainly accountable, but it isn't all your fault. And it's not her fault either.

"We've all been herded toward heterosexuality with no other acceptable alternatives. We've all tried to accommodate the lie that everyone is heterosexual, and lies lead to tragic messes like the way your marriage to Katelyn is ending. It's like driving off a cliff while denying the laws of gravity. The denial doesn't help anything. You still end up smashed at the bottom."

At least he decided to get his own lawyer. After the divorce, he continued to see me to help him with his coming-out process. As time passed, his connection with Katelyn became less contentious.

REFLECTIONS ON THE GAY HUSBAND

The main focus of this book is not "the gay husband," but I will summarize here some of the important information related to Jacob and Katelyn's story. See chapter 13 for helpful material on how couples can most constructively deal with a mixed-orientation marriage.

The question that Katelyn and most wives in her situation ask is, "Why didn't he know he was gay sooner, before we got married?" It can be a shock to a wife, unbelievable even, that her husband didn't know he was gay. But we have all been programmed not to see the signs of gayness in ourselves. Even today, homosexuality is stigmatized. Young people assume they are heterosexual and try to adapt themselves to it. Some gay teens who are feeling same-sex urges just hope they will go away, but often they're unaware they have them.

Most gay men who marry women truly fall in love with the women they marry. Why wouldn't they want a wife, children, and the American dream? It takes an effort of courageous self-awareness to accept that that dream is not for you.

How do these gay men keep themselves unaware of their identities? Some have a lot of promiscuous sex (with men or women, or both) to avoid dealing with their gay identity. Sex becomes their way of avoiding the issue. It also serves the same function as any other time-consuming addiction: a way of burning extra energy that might otherwise lead to introspection. On the other hand, some gay men who can't face their identities become asexual. Still others distract themselves from sex by throwing themselves into sports, work, or hobbies to suppress their unwanted impulses.

Often, gay men who are confused about their identities have no one to confide in, not even a priest, minister, or rabbi. Religious leaders commonly are not prepared to counsel on sexual orientation; they sometimes believe God doesn't approve of gays, and the only counseling they can offer are exhortations to self-discipline and silence. For this reason, gay men often find it difficult to find comfort in organized religion and support groups such as Alcoholics Anonymous, the way struggling straight people might. Without anyone to talk to, gay men live with their feelings and fears bottled up inside, impeding self-knowledge and facilitating denial.

It might take years for a man to know for sure that he is gay and wants to come out. He may not recognize his gayness until he falls in romantic love with another man. Unfortunately, this journey of self-discovery is usually taken privately; the wife has no forewarning.

Men can have sex with men without considering themselves gay; they just think of it as "alternative sexuality" or "flexibility." They think: *It's just what I do when I'm bored or alone or I travel or I drink or I drug or I'm mad at my wife, but it doesn't say anything about me. My identity is straight.* Later, looking back, they sometimes tell me, "I knew I was gay, but I couldn't let myself know it, so I kept telling myself that I was straight." Homophobia is a strong motivation to avoid being branded "gay."

A sexual identity includes all of the thoughts, feelings, fantasies, and emotions that cause a person to become sexually excited. Thus, the difference between a gay man and a straight man who has sex with men is distinct. But, if the stakes are high enough, humans are experts at self-deception.

Once a gay husband comes out to his wife, the relationship undergoes rapid changes. Many therapists see divorce as the only option, but this is shortsighted (or bigoted). It is not for the therapist (or anyone else) to decide whether a couple should stay together. The final decision is theirs. Chapter 13 discusses various options for mixed-orientation couples.

Whatever arrangements a mixed-orientation couple makes to accommodate the gay man, I believe personal integrity requires that these arrangements be open and honest, and in particular not kept as secrets from the wife. She, in turn, may have accommodations she would like to include in the negotiations. It is psychologically unhealthy not to be congruent with yourself from the inside out. Many couples I've worked with do choose to stay married for many reasons and work out a variety of different arrangements. For example, the gay spouse might have someone on the side or pursue sexual hookups outside the marriage with his wife's knowledge and agreement. I completely support a mixed-orientation couple staying together, as long as the marriage isn't grounded in desperation or lies.

As a couples therapist, it is not for me to decide whether a couple should stay together. The *final* decision is theirs. At one time, I thought that anything except monogamy was a betrayal of a committed relationship. I no longer believe that. However, I do strongly believe that whatever arrangements people make in relationships, the "rules" should be clearly stated and agreed upon by both parties. Neither should feel resentment or pressure. The fidelity of the man and woman is to their own agreement, not to some ancient set of commandments they do not wish to follow. "Sexual boundary agreements" are discussed in detail in chapter 15.

AFTER THE DIVORCE

Jacob and Katelyn bought their own homes. Katelyn met someone else; Jacob established himself in the gay community. They managed their joint custody gracefully. Sally and Megan were comfortable with their father as well as their mother.

Katelyn found her way to acceptance. She still loved this man, and she liked being connected to him. He never stopped loving her. They're both sorry that their marriage didn't work out, because they both wanted it to. They both had so wanted the perfect American family.

* * *

Sexual interests, sexual behavior, and sexual identity are different and are not always aligned in an individual. Some people are not that sexual; others are always horny. Some have a narrow range of sexual interests; others sample broadly. Some have good impulse control; others leap at every opportunity. The timid and cautious are shocked by those who will do anything with anybody. Some people feel they must express their true sexual identity, and this need is so important that suicide seems the only alternative.

This book has focused on straight guys who are interested in sex with men or who are inclined toward sexual interests some people believe are "gay." We've also considered the bisexual and the gay husband. In the next chapter, we'll summarize what the cases in part I tell us. It should be clear by now that a person's sexual behavior is highly individual and that "gay," "straight," and "bisexual" are only crude approximations of a much more fluid sexual reality.

9

A LANDSCAPE OF IDENTITY AND DESIRE

Straight Men Who Seem Gay

There is no sexual potential in an identity rooted in denial of possibility.

—Laurie Essig[1]

How do we understand gay, straight, and bisexual? This chapter summarizes and clarifies the two major themes that emerge from the stories in part I.

First, a man may be straight but have sexual fantasies or behaviors that seem gay. He may feel compelled to have sex with men. He may be drawn to kinks that look gay but do not involve sex with men. Sometimes therapy will reveal the cause of the behavior. Sometimes the cause will remain unknown.

The second major theme is that the very concept of sexual identity is far more complicated and confusing than a few simply defined categories. The primitive idea that "if you're a man who has sex with men, you're gay or bi" is not true. A man's sexual identity and desire are part of a complex and subtle landscape that is shaped by his nature and his history.

MEN WHO "ACT GAY" BUT MOSTLY AREN'T

The stories we've considered in part I illustrate a variety of situations and options. Tom, from chapters 1 and 2, sought sex with men, but the reason why was the abuse he suffered at the hands of his coach when he was a child. He was "acting out" the sexual abuse. Getting therapy made him less compulsive, and most likely he will never have sex with men again, because he wasn't interested in having sex with men at all. His behavior had been driven entirely by what psychologists call "trauma reenactment." Tom's case illustrates the value of having a careful psychological intervention to clarify the couple's options. It revealed the cause of his acting out and confirmed that he did not have a gay or bi identity. Therapy lifted the weight of his compulsion and let him claim his own sexuality. He and Jennifer were able to repair and reestablish their marriage.

Joel, in chapter 3, was obsessed with a cuckolding fantasy. The fantasy itself is common and harmless, but Joel was engaging in compulsive and risky behaviors that motivated us to uncover the origins and diminish the force of the compulsions. Joel did not have a gay or bi identity. Even though a man played a role in Joel's fantasy, he was not turned on by men. Instead, we discovered a trauma in Joel's childhood that was defining and driving his acting out. The trauma was not sexual abuse but a complex situation in which his mother was intensely loving when his father was away but ignored him totally when his father was present. This chronic inconsistency about something as fundamental as a mother's love set the parameters of his core sexual scripts and charged them with a compulsive energy. He had "eroticized the pain" he had felt as a child, the humiliation of "when Daddy's home, you're nothing." His acting out was another example of trauma reenactment, Tom's resulting from abuse and Joel's from abandonment. Although therapy didn't make his fantasies go away entirely—core sexual scripts never go away—their compulsive nature was diminished significantly. (See chapter 11 on core sexual scripts.) He could keep them under control so that they no longer threatened the stability of his marriage.

A particular aspect of kinks is that shame about the kink can cause considerable damage. Shame turbocharges a kink, making it that much more likely to lead to compulsive behaviors. This is an important distinction. A "turn-on" doesn't have to rule your life, but a compulsion can take it over entirely. Although I take seriously the need to treat and control sexual addictions and other compulsive and destructive behaviors, I generally believe it is more helpful for clients with kinks to find safe outlets for them than to try to contain them with total abstinence.

I'm always surprised that anal sex is controversial and in particular is considered the exclusive provenance of gay men. Nothing about anal is gay. David, in chapter 4, was a little more focused on it than are most men, but all men are biologically inclined to enjoy anal stimulation. David learned that he didn't have to go to extremes to hide his interest from his wife, Judith. He was shocked and moved that she was willing to try it. Their story illustrates how trust and love can turn what look like insurmountable obstacles into small challenges that a couple can conquer together.

In chapter 5 we discovered that BDSM can lead to an identity that is so compelling it may destroy a marriage. Adam needed to live out his sense of himself as a "master," and Cynthia couldn't live with that. It was easy to determine that he wasn't gay, even though he had "played" BDSM scenes with a man. The experience of "hard play" with someone who happened to be a man had showed Adam how strong his BDSM identity really was. He would have preferred to play with women, but the role of master was more important to him than the gender of his slave. Adam and Cynthia were unable to resolve his commitment to BDSM and her rejection of it, and divorce followed.

It is not always possible or necessary to uncover a "cause" for troubling sexual thoughts or behaviors. Carlos, in chapter 6, was suffering from extreme psychological anxiety to the point that his fear of being homosexual was diagnosable as an obsessive-compulsive disorder (OCD). His homosexual OCD was endangering his dream of marrying Anna, the love of his life. When I examined him, he did not exhibit the characteristics of a gay or bi man. The reason for his HOCD wasn't clear, but he responded well to treatment, which included therapy and medication. He and Anna did eventually marry.

Bisexual men live in terrible isolation. The gay community doesn't accept them. Gay men commonly assume a bisexual man is a gay man coming out. Straight people often assume the same. Yet, a man with a bisexual identity needs to be affirmed by his peer group just as much as gay men do. Most wives are understandably not comfortable allowing a bisexual husband to have "sex on the side." In chapter 7, Sam was married to Jillian. He was in love with her and wanted to stay married, but over their eight years of marriage, he "came out" as bi and felt the need to act on it. He was scrupulously honest with Jillian, and after a great deal of agonizing, pleading, and arguing, she allowed him to explore. It doesn't always work out like this, but in Sam's case a relatively short period of exploration allowed him to confirm his bi identity and at the same time allowed him to "settle down" with Jillian. Sam's case follows a pattern I see often: A bi man lives out a period of "bi adolescence" and then can choose to be faithful to one partner. However, other bi men who want to be married to a woman feel the need to be actively connected indefinitely in various ways to the gay male community. In my experience, many wives are uncomfortable with this, and (unfortunately) many married bisexual men choose to keep their bisexuality secret from their wives.

Jacob, in chapter 8, was unambiguously gay. He loved Katelyn, and they had two young children, but he simply had to live out his gay identity. Although some mixed-orientation couples can make practical arrangements that allow them to stay together, many do not. Divorce was not Jacob and Katelyn's only option, but it was a reasonable choice under the circumstances. Chapter 13 discusses mixed-orientation couples.

Tom, Joel, David, Adam, and Carlos are men with sexual interests or behaviors that appear to make them gay, but none of them has a gay or bi sexual identity. The issue of identity is pivotal here, because the options and outcomes change enormously for mixed-orientation marriages with a gay husband.

Let's spend a little time clarifying identity, because it is such a confusing and misunderstood concept.

WHO YOU ARE, NOT WHAT YOU DO

Identity requires affirmation from a peer group. It requires community. A gay person can have all kinds of sex in the closet, but it isn't enough. "Affirmation of identity" is "mirroring of who a person is at his or her core" by people who have the same core.

The confusions are many. One is of "sex that affirms identity" as opposed to "sex for itself." This distinction is not that hard to understand. Many people know "sex for approval" and understand that it is different from "sex for pleasure." And, especially, a straight man who has sex with men because he is reenacting childhood trauma isn't seeking affirmation or pleasure or approval. He has a little bit of connection with his sex partners in the moment, but when the sex is over, he feels only guilt and shame and a compulsive need to repeat the scene. He doesn't feel the affirmation that he would feel if he were gay or bi.

A gay guy needs to "homosocialize." He needs to feel his gayness mirrored in a community of other men who will help him express it, joke about it, talk about it, have brotherhood around it. It's like what every straight boy wants when he's going through his peer-group stage: "We're a bunch of guys and we feed each other's masculine souls by sharing how much we're into girls." Gay boys need the same thing but often lose that opportunity when they are children; consequently, they often feel overwhelmed by isolation and depression. The affirmation is that important.

Of course, gay introverts do not so easily find social affirmation of their gayness, but a gay loner can receive the affirmation of his peer group indirectly, through articles in the newspaper, magazines, and online; in books, movies, and TV shows; and, yes, in pornography. From these, he can sense that he is recognized as a brother, as a member of the family, as one of the good guys.

We've been talking about gay men, but what we've been considering applies to women, to bisexuals, to straight people, to everybody. The phenomenon of identity comes up everywhere. Two Jews living in a gentile community love to meet and acknowledge each other. Examples abound across religious, racial, occupational, and ethnic lines. Identity has biological and sociological roots, not always clearly distinguished. Siblings separated by war or poverty meet and know each other. Identity includes some sort of mysterious cellular awareness. Much has been written on this topic. We are merely reminding ourselves here of some of its elements.

Thus, bisexual men also have a distinct identity that needs acknowledgment, but bisexual identity has been less discussed and described in the popular press and among professional psychologists in recent decades. It used to be that I would always talk "gay" or "straight," and not really acknowledge bisexuality. Only in the past five years have I started looking at bisexuality, considering it seriously, recognizing its reality. The more I've learned, the more I see that the many shades of bisexuality are real. Dr. Kinsey acknowledged this in *Sexual Behavior in the Human Male*[2] more than sixty years ago via his "seven-point scale," now called the "Kinsey scale." He assigned 0 (zero) to totally straight men and 6 to totally gay men. The numbers 1 through 5 quantify shades of gayness from "mostly straight" to "mostly gay" in five gradations. The topic of bisexuality is vast and beyond the scope of this book, but see *The Bisexual Option*.[3]

Sexual pursuits not grounded in identity do not carry the core of need of sexual pursuits grounded in identity. This need seems to be especially intense if an individual's ability to express his or her identity has been blocked in the past. On the other hand, a sexual identity acknowledged in adolescence—or at least acknowledged in some period of late adolescence—may carry less life-or-death intensity. It's been satiated, acknowledged, confirmed. The identity will always be there; the way it must be expressed will include more options.

Identity can't be changed by therapy. In the past, some reparative therapists have confused traumatic reenactment of childhood abuse with a gay identity. When the trauma was treated, the compulsive sexual behavior was defused and a mistaken "change of sexual identity" claimed. These therapists mostly have come to understand their mistake, and less and less of this sort of "change of identity" is being talked about today.

The gay husband's motive for "straying" is often to find his true identity. Of course, this exploration should have been allowed during his adolescence and young-adult years. A wife should be aware that the cheating is not about her husband's inability to love and bond with her. Nor is it generally the result of marital problems. Typically, a wife feels she did something to cause her gay husband to seek affairs with men. Therapists can help straight spouses stop blaming themselves for their partners' wanderings and encourage them to avoid concluding that something was wrong with the marriage itself.

WHAT NOW?

Less than 20 percent of mixed-orientation marriages with a gay-male husband survive the trauma of the man's coming out. Thus, Jacob and Katelyn divorced, despite their love for one another, their children, their hard-won place in the American dream. The expectations for a marriage with a bisexual husband are more complicated. Sam and Jillian managed to stay together after considerable stress and difficulty. In chapter 13, we consider the full range of possibilities in managing a mixed-orientation marriage. If a husband (or fiancé) is gay or bi, then his identity will put stress on the marriage because of his possible need to homosocialize, which may be a necessary part of the affirmation of his identity. If the wife can tolerate a partly open marriage, then the need to divorce may be less compelling, although societal pressure to separate still will be very strong.

If *identity* is not the issue, then the couple has a more flexible range of options. Although identity can't be modified by therapy, other issues often can be. For example, therapy can be a powerful tool in reducing the force of compulsions driven by childhood abuse or neglect. After a successful course of therapy has given the man more control over his compulsions and impulses, I often find myself suggesting a "porn open marriage" in which the man is allowed porn and fantasies, but he agrees not to meet or contact other sex partners. (Chapter 12 focuses on kinks and how to manage them.) A person's behavior is much more adaptable than his core sexual scripts, which are often as fixed as identity. (Chapter 11 discusses the significance of core sexual scripts.) Having safe sexual outlets is often a practical way to balance reality with the needs of a stable relationship.

Is the ideal to share all your sex fantasies with your partner? No. In fact, it's often a bad idea, for reasons discussed in chapter 14.

Chapter 15 focuses narrowly on establishing sexual boundaries when the marriage has had a problem with boundary violations. We understand that a man and woman together will have many other needs to negotiate, and I strongly recommend the Imago approach to bringing couples together, as described in chapter 15. The spirit of the narrow focus of *Is My Husband Gay, Straight, or Bi?* is to respond to the 911 call of a couple in crisis and stabilize the marriage before it expires. The broader health of the relationship can be addressed after the initial panic has subsided.

Chapter 16 considers straight men in sexual situations with men—not always "having sex" with men—and the range of reasons and motivations that lead them there. Some of these situations require urgent therapy, but others are mere ripples in the great ocean of human sexual variety and require nothing more than an appreciation that human sexual nature is never as simple as we think.

Fifty percent of marriages end it divorce. The reasons vary. The main message of this book is that a couple always has options. Despite the statistics and despite some pundits' declarations to the contrary, no marriage is doomed by circumstance to end in divorce.

* * *

The shock of discovering a man's hidden sexual interests will always be traumatic, but dealing with such trauma can be an opportunity to grow. In the next chapter, we'll see that healing and restoring trust are always possible.

II

What Can You Do?

10

HIS SECRET SEX LIFE

Recovering from Betrayal

Finding his porn was like finding him in bed with another woman.[1]

Let's imagine the following situation. You and your husband have been married for ten years. You enjoy sex with him; he enjoys it with you. You think the two of you are on the same page.

Then, you discover something out of the ordinary that catches your attention, and you innocently pursue it to find out what's up. You might see a text message, a porn site, an e-mail, or maybe some irregularity in your husband's schedule. You ask what's going on, and he answers with a fumbled and awkward reply that confuses you more than it clears things up. Immediately and intuitively, you know your partner is lying, but a part of you doesn't want to believe it.

So you let that go, but you begin looking for other clues that might give you more information. Maybe you find other bits and pieces, and your husband consistently (and sometimes, implausibly) denies everything. You start to feel crazy. You can't nail down anything, and you desperately want to believe him. You feel guilty that you are being so suspicious. *I'm not usually like this*, you tell yourself. But you can't help it. You find yourself going through phone bills or putting locators on his phone, maybe even hiring a private investigator. All along, you're asking yourself, *What is wrong with me that I can't trust my husband?* And he keeps telling you that nothing's going on.

Whatever you find, he denies. "No, that's not me in that photograph. No, I have no idea where that pair of underpants came from. No, I never sent that e-mail." You walk into a room, and he quickly changes his computer screen; or you notice he's answering texts and e-mails with his phone turned away from you. You mention something about it, only to have him say things such as, "What's wrong with you that you don't trust me?" or "Something is wrong with you if you think I'd go to those porn sites." You so want to believe him. Better that you are going crazy than that the man you love is betraying you.

You want to believe him, but you keep finding things. We call this process of denying your reality and making you feel crazy "gaslighting." The term comes from a movie, *Gaslight*, where a husband tries to drive his wife insane by manipulating what's happening around her and denying that anything has changed. Betrayed women need to know the term "gaslight" so they can understand that it's not their fault that they feel suspicious and crazy. And their men need to be held accountable for the tremendous psychological harm they cause by doing this.

THE SHOCK OF THE LIE

The moment comes when you can no longer ignore the truth. Maybe you've confronted him, and he's finally confessed. Maybe the evidence is overwhelming, and you no longer care what he says about it. You finally are sure there is a major aspect of his sexuality that you've never heard of, never even imagined. It could be anything: He might be having sex with men or meeting couples for sexual games, such as cuckolding. He might be meeting a guy so they can masturbate to porn. He might be staying home but acting out sexually on the Internet via sexual chat rooms or porn sites. Whatever it is, you didn't know about it. Whatever the details are, the shock is that he wasn't telling you about it. He has been having a secret sex life.

You feel betrayed. You feel angry. You feel scared, mortified, and sad. Your world is turned upside down. You don't know what to do.

First of all, I want to tell you that your feelings are reasonable. They are justified. Your man has hidden from you a major part of his life.

Now that you know, you're probably going through a lot of reactions. You're taking it personally. You're disoriented. What do these crazy sexual things mean about your husband? Is he gay? Is he a dangerous pervert? What's going on?

DEALING WITH THE CRISIS

When a couple comes into my office in the aftermath of such a devastating discovery, it's often because the wife has told her husband, "You'd better get help, or I'm leaving." I do individual therapy with the man to discover what's going on for him. We have to figure him out. We have to understand where his behavior is coming from and where it is heading, because it will make a big difference if he has a gay or bi orientation; if he is acting out a sexual compulsion due to childhood trauma; or if he is being driven by a kink buried deep in his core sexual scripts. The details matter. Powerful fantasies, interests, and behaviors need to be understood and clarified. If he is gay or bi, then you and he are dealing with the compelling requirements and obligations of sexual orientation and identity. This is why I recommend when I'm meeting with the couple that I do individual therapy with the man, The following two chapters (11 and 12) describe some of the major themes he and I discuss.

However, I understand that you need to express how it feels to be so betrayed. What could be worse than having your trust undermined in this way? You counted on him to be honest with you, and now you know he's been lying to you for years.

Typically, even while I am helping your man in individual therapy sort out his sexual situation, I'll spend time in my office with both of you, so that you can let him hear how what he's done feels to you. He's hurt you. He's broken your heart. You may feel you'll never be the same. You may feel you'll never be able to trust again. And he needs to hear how you feel about all that. He needs to listen to your pain and heartache. No healing can happen in your relationship until he hears the truth from you. You deserve to be listened to. You deserve to have your feelings witnessed and validated.

As I'm working with you as a couple and him individually, I will strongly recommend that you get your own individual therapy—either with me or another therapist—to deal with the impact of all of this on you. Many women I've counseled have found two books especially helpful: *After the Affair: Healing the Pain and Rebuilding Trust When a*

Partner Has Been Unfaithful[2] and *Mending a Shattered Heart: A Guide for Partners of Sex Addicts.*[3] The second book includes my chapter for a wife who discovers her husband has been having sex with men.

Most men find it very difficult to listen to the sadness and anger they have caused. I generally have to teach a man that it is his job to listen, to be patient and validate by acknowledging what his wife is telling him. This is not to say that she can choose any time and any length of time to punish her man with her words and her feelings. I have seen this happen, especially at the beginning of therapy. I teach them both to set time limits and talk only when both are ready and willing to do so without overreacting, with the understanding that a time within twenty-four hours of the request generally is expected.

You may find it unbelievable, but essentially he may be clueless about the damage he's done. A man caught in the fog of a sexual addiction or compulsion may simply not be thinking about the consequences of his actions. He's disassociated and separated his life into the acting-out part and the part with you. But he was aware enough to be secretive. He wasn't telling you, because he wanted to avoid your reactions. He knew you wouldn't approve. He knew you were going to be shocked. More than anything, he didn't want to hurt you. In his mind, not telling you was protecting you. Also, he may simply have been ashamed of what he was doing.

THE HEALING PROCESS—AN OVERVIEW

When you learn of your husband's secret sexual life, you are typically mortified. You can't imagine a more significant betrayal. It is often your impulse to go into your own tunnel of secrets, not to want to talk about it, not to want anybody to find out about it. That's very natural. Therapists counseling mixed-orientation couples have this saying: *When he comes out of the closet, she goes into it.* But you shouldn't have to stay silent. You need a support person—a sister, a brother, a friend, and not just the therapist—to whom you can talk. This is your secret, too, and it's not fair to make you be quiet about it. By the time I meet a betrayed wife, if she has not told anyone, she is very distraught. She feels awful, and I let her know, "You need to tell somebody. It's okay. Find yourself a confidant."

Of course, I always advise couples in this situation to talk with each other and to listen to each other. I offer guidance and counseling to help make the whole painful process as healing as possible.

You must start by airing the facts and the feelings. A willingness to be honest and to speak with integrity is called for. It is the first step—a big step—but it must happen. After some time passes and we can move forward, we address the deeper questions of motivations and root causes. I work with your man, along the lines I've mentioned above and outline in the next two chapters, to clarify what has caused him to behave the way he has.

A woman caught up in her husband's sexual issues cannot help but take it personally, even if logic tells her it's his issue, not hers. You ask yourself, *What does this say about me?* You think, *This is about me. I should have been more of a woman. A better wife. A better sexual partner.* Usually, none of this is true, but it is very natural to think so.

"Did I make him gay?" is a question I'm often asked, if it turns out he is gay. Or "Did I make him turn to porn or kinky sex or sex with men?" No matter what their husbands are dealing with sexually, women do tend to blame themselves.

It is also very natural for you to be angry. You want to say (and maybe you did say) to your husband, "What's wrong with you? What did I marry? Some pervert? Some pathological liar?" You can't help but be very angry.

Because sharing strong feelings is very confronting and potentially more damaging than helpful, it's probably best done in a therapist's office. But one way or another, it must be done. As long as you hold on to your hurt feelings, it will be difficult to find your way past bitterness and blame. Yet, despite the difficulties, I've seen many couples move beyond the first shock of discovery to find that their relationship can be repaired and made even better.

It wouldn't surprise me, after your husband has begun therapy, if you want to know, or even manage, every detail of his therapy work. "Are you going? What are you saying? What are you doing? Tell me what happened in your session." You'll be trying to help, but this micromanaging isn't good for either of you, or your relationship. It's not healthy for you, and I'm sure you really don't want to do it.

I expect that, over time, you will move toward acceptance and learn to stop taking the situation personally, but it can take time—two years, even five years. At some point, you begin to see that you had nothing to do with your husband's core sexual issues. It never was about the marriage. You overcome the notion that he knew everything about himself when he married you, and, therefore, he deceived you. In my experience, most men marry before they understand themselves sexually, whatever their issues. They think their gayness, kinky fantasies, or compulsions are only a stage, only about sex, or will go away once they are married.

After you feel heard and validated around the pain this has caused you, you most likely will be able to find some serenity. You may have already benefited from your individual therapy. Now you can make room for listening to his story and feel less compelled to manage his recovery. As you come to understand what your husband is dealing with, and as he makes progress in his own therapy, you will discover in yourself the ability to reestablish trust in your marriage and in him.

If you discover you're having significant long-term reactions to his sexual acting out, it would most likely be best for you to talk about that in your individual therapy. Upon reflection, you may recognize that you came from a childhood where sexual boundaries were blurred either from sexual abuse, parental affairs, or something dysfunctional in your home, leading you to choose a partner with sexual issues. The connection is unconscious, but one that makes sense after you reflect on your life and think about why you married the man you did. For example, in chapter 2 we learned that the grief Jennifer's mother expressed over her father's affair inflamed Jennifer's reaction to Tom's behavior. And if you have any sexual issues from the past, they almost always surface when your marriage is troubled, and they become a part of the problem that needs to be healed and resolved in the present.

The Imago approach to couples therapy (described briefly in chapter 15) specifically assumes that you chose a partner to help you heal old wounds; in other words, a partner whose issues would evoke your issues so that both of you would be forced to face the unfinished healing you need.

However, the biggest problems you will have are the same problems women always have when their husbands have cheated: loss of trust, feelings of betrayal, shock at unimagined secrets and deceit. You should try to address in your therapy all of these things. Even after therapy, for years after, you may still have moments where you discover you are feeling the old pain again. These "betrayal flashbacks" are normal and should be acknowledged when they occur with respectful listening by your husband and additional therapy, if necessary.

Sadly, some women feel victimized and never recover. I am always concerned that a wife's anger, while justified, will become part of her life narrative rather than pass through her. I've seen this when a woman has a lifetime of past injustices and injuries. The "cheating spouse" becomes the container for all the pain and hurt of her life. Of course, this is not exclusive to women; men do it, too.

A few angry wives I've met have built their lives around being the victims of their "sicko" husbands. It's okay to "be a victim" for a while, because you have been victimized, but if that becomes who you are, your identity, that's a sad place to end up. I urge all the wives I counsel to find a more healing path.

MOVING ON—CHOOSING TO BE A VICTOR RATHER THAN A VICTIM

You need to accept that your old relationship is gone. Your man will not "go back" to being the man you thought he was. You will not go back to being the wife you were. Often, a stronger relationship can be built on the ruins of the old. That's not a bad thing. That's a good thing. Instead of having "assumed trust" in your marriage, now you will have the opportunity to build "earned trust" between the two of you around sexual matters. It is an opportunity to be clearer about what your marriage contract says about sex.

Even if your marriage ends, you will benefit from self-knowledge. You didn't just happen across a man who betrayed you. It's about how you chose this man to have a relationship with.

This may be where you want to throw down the book and never pick it up again. That's a normal reaction. It may feel like I'm blaming you and saying you're the problem. I'm not. I am saying this: If you don't look at your piece, too, then you'll do this again. You'll leave this relationship a victim and not a victor. Your experience won't empower you at all. It will just leave you in this dusty, mysterious "how did this happen to me" state of mind instead of "what was my contribution to making this happen, and how can I avoid it in the future?"

You have control over your choices, only yours and nobody else's. To survive is a victory if you make better choices going forward. Most women I counsel are in this sense victorious. You can be, too.

* * *

In chapters 11 and 12, we'll look at the different things that may compel a man to pursue a secret sexual life; and with this understanding, we will be able to consider the opportunities for making things better as outlined in chapters 13, 14, and 15.

11

CORE SEXUAL SCRIPTS

Gateway to Understanding Troubling Sexual Behavior

Tell me how you were loved as a child, and I will tell you how you make love as an adult.

—Esther Perel[1]

Everybody has one or more personal favored sexual fantasies, which we have been calling core sexual scripts (CSS). These are created in childhood in the same way for everyone from significant feelings and events, not necessarily negative, often not sexual. When these early feelings and events are happy, the resulting core sexual scripts will often be untroubled. However, trouble in childhood (as well as later) may be revealed in a troubled CSS.

When a person comes to therapy with sexual issues, I will generally look into his or her sexual fantasies for clues to the origins of the trouble. The CSS of my clients will often reveal the key issues they need to address. Thus, a man in the grip of sexual compulsions can gain relief by learning what is driving his behavior, and his partner can gain a more empathetic understanding of what he is dealing with.

Even a person who is not sexually troubled can gain insights by studying his or her sexual fantasies. Imprints from childhood that link to adult behaviors can be gleaned by sorting out the nonsexual meanings of core sexual scripts.

Core sexual scripts (CSS)—People have favored sexual fantasies: what they think about when they masturbate, what they imagine when they have erotic daydreams, what they see when they watch porn. We call the set of a person's favored fantasies their CSS. CSS often "retell" or "encode" past experiences, including significant childhood experiences.

WHAT'S GOING ON?

A couple comes into my office. The man has been engaging in sexual behavior that causes his wife or him (or both) to worry that he might be gay. How do I proceed? As described in chapter 10, I first help the wife deal with her sense of betrayal and the shock of her husband's unexpected sexual interests and behaviors. Soon, however, we must consider the nature of the man's sexuality. What is motivating his behavior?

These couples always ask me two things: First, why is he behaving this way? Is he being compelled for some psychological reason? Second, can I help him change his behavior? These sorts of questions are complicated to address, and in this chapter I explain what is involved in attempting to answer them.

I determine fairly soon in the therapeutic process if the man is gay or bisexual. If he *is* either of these, then the couple is dealing with the issues of a mixed-orientation marriage, or relationship, if they are not married. (As usual, I commonly refer to the couple as if they are married, even though I intend this book to be for any serious relationship.) We consider mixed-orientation marriages in detail in chapter 13. Here, we consider the situation that the man is neither gay nor bi. As we have seen in part I, his behavior may seem to be gay, but that doesn't mean he has a gay (or bi) orientation. What I want to do for the couple in this case is to help discover what is driving the man's sexual behavior and interests.

The process I use is to work with the man to determine the nonsexual meanings of his sexual fantasies and interests. The resulting insights will give him relief and greater control and will give his wife increased understanding and empathy. I have seen couples who thought they had an intractable issue come together after this process with greater love and connectedness than they'd ever had before.

WHY WOULD A STRAIGHT MAN LIKE GAY PORN?

George and his wife, Susan, came to see me. Susan had discovered in George's online history that he liked to watch gay medical porn. She was worried that he might be gay.

In gay medical porn, two male actors play doctor and patient, and the doctor gets sexual with the patient. Although George wasn't compulsive with his porn—he didn't spend an unreasonable amount of time or money on it—he did enjoy watching it occasionally. He didn't think this was a problem, but Susan was very upset.

"If he's looking at gay porn," she told me, "he must be gay."

So I worked with him in individual therapy. I asked him, "Why do you look at this kind of porn?"

"I don't know," was his honest answer.

So, as I always do when someone has troubling sexual fantasies about which we'd like more insight, I questioned him about the details of his fantasies. Exactly what about medical porn turned him on?

I began with questions to help decide if he were gay or bi. I did my usual screening, but all of his answers were those of a straight man. I asked a few follow-up questions to make sure.

"Are you sexually attracted to either man in the porn? Do you see yourself in the position of the doctor or the patient? Or both?" I asked him.

"No. I'm not attracted to the men."

"So why do you watch it?"

"I don't know. There's just something about it. I imagine I'm the patient. It's the situation I'm in."

"What do you like about the situation?" I asked him.

He'd never thought about it systematically, but he had a ready answer. "I'm aroused by the doctor crossing the line. I like that the patient is willing to go along."

He made a point of telling me that he enjoyed this fantasy, but he would be appalled if it happened in reality.

"What if the doctor were a woman?" I asked him.

"Nope," he said. "In all the porn I watch, the doctor is a man."

After some weeks of consideration of his fantasy and his history, we discovered a fact he'd "forgotten": his male doctor had sexually abused him when he was a boy. In fact, this doctor had abused all the boys in the neighborhood.

This kind of abuse sometimes leads to serious adult compulsive sexual behavior, sexual addiction, or other behaviors with significant consequences, as we saw in chapters 1 and 2. This didn't happen to George. He did carry a sadness, a depression, but not a debilitating one, and he was drawn to the porn. This porn provided a "happy ending" to what had felt very hurtful to him when he was a child. By "happy ending," I mean that in the porn story everyone is having a good time, and all the people are pleasuring each other. (I should note that the porn showed only adult actors.) In the real sexual abuse, only the perpetrator (the doctor) was happy, especially in enjoying his power and control over the boys, who were victimized and felt no good feelings. George's use of this porn may have been helping him "contain" his depression.

It is important to point out that many people have sexual fantasies about things that they would never want to do in reality. These things may be harmful or even illegal. However, in sexual fantasies they become things to "play" with. Having such a fantasy does not mean that a person is inclined in reality to do the harmful things in the fantasy.

So now George and I could reassure Susan. George explained that he had been sexually abused by his doctor when he was a boy, and his interest in the medical porn seemed to come from that. I told her that her husband and I were going to do therapy around the sadness and grief and the loss he felt and the sense of betrayal he was carrying from boyhood. He was suffering from psychological trauma.

Psychological Trauma—Psychological trauma (often just called "trauma") is a type of damage to the mind that occurs from a severely distressing event or collection of events. The traumatic event or events completely overwhelm the individual's ability to cope with the ideas and emotions evoked. The symptoms of trauma can be overlooked for weeks, years, or even decades. Trauma victims can organize much of their lives around distressing repetitive patterns of reliving and warding off the traumatic memories, reminders, and feelings. Typical causes of psychological trauma are sexual abuse, bullying, violence, neglect, verbal abuse, and being threatened by or witnessing any of these, particularly in childhood. However, different people react differently to similar events. One person may experience an event as extremely traumatic, whereas another person would not suffer significant trauma from the same event. In other words, people who experience a traumatic event will not become psychologically traumatized to the same degree.

This concept of trauma is not a simple one. In George's case, a violation of trust in childhood by someone who was supposed to be safe caused George to "upload an emotional charge" that became locked in his psychological system. He had no way to release it other than the porn. This type of "charge" can cause a multitude of problems (depression, sexual acting out) until the original traumatic event can be talked about and explicitly felt with all of its grief and anger. A child generally has no one to tell and has no choice but to keep the story to himself or herself and let the poison of it fester.

I explained to George and Susan that his therapy work would no doubt make him a happier man, but it might not take away his interest in gay medical porn. It might, but it might not.

"In either case," I asked Susan, "can you have compassion and empathy for George, now that you know his interest is a symptom of his childhood abuse? It isn't about his being gay. He isn't gay. The fantasy in and of itself is not a threat to you. It's not going to compete with you. But it may never go away either."

Susan was okay with this. Now that she understood, she felt less of a need for George to give up his porn. It was no longer that big a deal to her.

GIVING A NONSEXUAL VOICE TO A SEXUAL NARRATIVE

So, consider that a man's sexual behavior has caused him or his wife trouble and made them believe he might be gay, but we find he's not gay or bi. Then, my starting point for understanding and giving him mastery and control over his sexual behaviors is to work with him to clarify and understand the nonsexual meaning of his core sexual scripts. The key idea here is that within the man's favored sexual fantasies are encoded the nonsexual stories that are making his sexual behavior so troubling.

I describe this process as "giving a nonsexual voice to the man's sexual narrative." Almost always, the resulting insights and understandings significantly alleviate the impairment the man was experiencing because of his sexual interests and behaviors. He has more control and choice. He is less compulsive. He has less shame.

It has been long understood that sexual fantasies contain significant nonsexual meaning. Two books I particularly like develop this connection in great detail: *Arousal: The Secret Logic of Sexual Fantasies*[2] and *The Erotic Mind: Unlocking the Inner Sources of Sexual Passion and Fulfillment*.[3] These books describe how people can learn about themselves by considering the meanings of their sexual fantasies, even if no particular psychological problem needs to be addressed.

HOW THE PAST HARMS THE PRESENT AND HOW THERAPY HEALS IT

Those who influenced us when we were growing up had positive and negative traits. Our caretakers imprinted us with their care and with their neglect, with their love and with their abuse, so as adults we're compelled and drawn to aspects of what feels familiar from our childhoods. However, the negative traits of our caretakers are more indelibly imprinted in us, because those traits caused the most painful experiences. The imprinting by our caretakers, especially the hurtful and shameful experiences, is strongly reflected in our CSS.

I often say that a part of you is "returning to the scene of the sexual crime, trying to solve the crime by setting it up all over again." The problem is that this part of you knows only how to set the scene, not how to solve the crime.

The bad things that happened in childhood may be events (e.g., rape) or situations (e.g., chronically absent parents) that we naturally hold inside us as stories. These are the stories that we "act out" when we seek a favored type of sexual encounter. Ironically, the sex that makes the bad feelings of the past feel better also blocks the process that allows the wounds to heal.

In the therapeutic process, a client becomes aware of the nonsexual meaning of the stories that have been "coming up" for him or her as sexual fantasies. Each fantasy is a mask, and behind the mask is the real story, the historic event or situation that the fantasy simultaneously tells and hides. After the client can see behind the mask of the fantasy, then the nonsexual meaning, the traumatic situation or negative memory from childhood, becomes attached to the fantasy. Once the client makes this connection, the therapy can help resolve the original incident, removing the compulsive need to reenact it through sexual behavior. This "therapeutic resolving" of the original incident includes feeling and expressing the sadness and the grief from the past wound, which cannot be resolved until it is felt and expressed. Also, understanding the original trauma can enhance the empathy and remove the shame of the man for himself and of his wife for him.

> The sex that makes the bad feelings of the past feel better also blocks the process that allows the wounds to heal.

The workings of the unconscious mind are very difficult to explain. Therapists generally use the following sort of metaphor. Imagine that a "younger you" inside you shares your body but cannot directly communicate with you. This part of you remembers certain kinds of pain from the past, and its need to "tell the story" is enormous. It has a strange way of getting your attention. It causes you to hurt yourself. Its intention is not to hurt you but to help you, but this part is so young it doesn't know how to help. You wonder why you are hurting yourself, yet you can't stop. Imagine a drinking or eating or sexual addiction. The adult you won't be able to stop the younger you until it is allowed to tell its story more directly. The telling of the story is accomplished through therapy. Generally, it is very difficult to open this channel of communication to the unconscious mind without the aid of a therapist. The pain from the past is too loaded with taboos. It is too charged with strong feelings. Generally, too much homophobia is there, too much sexual misunderstanding, for a person, or a couple, to be able to find their way without a trained guide.

Some therapists speak of an "inner child," especially because the pain from the past is often (early) childhood pain. We might talk of being "stuck in the past" or being "stuck at the age of five." When you were hurt as a child but could not express your hurt, a remnant of you as that child at that time remains in you. Let's suppose some special hurt happened when you were five. Then, a part of you is "stuck back at five," and this part keeps reenacting in your present life the story of its five-year-old hurt. This happens in a kind of code, so that the events of the past are transformed when they are acted out (as sexual behavior) in the present. The hurt is eroticized, and it doesn't hurt so much anymore.

Still, if you allow this five-year-old to control your sexual behavior, the "adult you" will not be in control of it, and many kinds of trouble will follow. A five-year-old doesn't know how to navigate an adult life or sexuality. So, therapy aims to soothe the five-year-old and convince him that he need not tell his story in this sexual way anymore.

How does this therapeutic process work? The therapy proceeds by acknowledging what happened to you at five, letting you feel some of the victimization of what happened. You were five. You weren't in control. You *were* powerless when your father did the bad thing to you. Partly, you excused your father. Partly, you explained your father, but a part of you is angry with him. Some of you is resentful of him. And much of you is ashamed of what he did to you. All of it is okay to feel. That's the psychotherapy: feeling the grief, the loss, the pain, the shame, and ultimately the acceptance of what happened. As you go back to yourself at five and offer comfort to the five-year-old, his need to seek comfort by making you act out sexually can be controlled by the adult you.

Psychotherapy helps a person uncover pain from the past, feel and express the associated feelings, and thereby free him or her from having to act out the pain in harmful ways. The result is a person who can make healthier adult choices.

The success of therapy to quiet this inner child who needs to tell its story, and in that way free someone from addictions or other destructive behaviors, can seem miraculous, perhaps even unlikely. But it does work. I help people using therapy every day.

I speak of control, mastery, and understanding, but I need to emphasize that neither control nor understanding will be perfect even if the therapy is very successful. Inevitably, a remnant of the unhealthy behavior will need to be managed into the future. However, the difference for the sufferer before and after therapy can be enormous. Even "imperfect" therapy can change a desperately unhappy and dysfunctional life into one that is relatively happy and functional.

THE STAGES OF THE CSS THERAPEUTIC PROCESS

I proceed with therapy in six stages. First, my client is encouraged to clarify his or her troubling sexual behavior or interests. Then, we explore favored masturbation fantasies and erotic daydreams to reveal the details of the CSS. Third, I get a family and social history and then (fourth) begin the process of connecting the CSS to nonsexual stories or situations from the past (perhaps a troubling relationship with a parent or any of a number of formative situations). As these nonsexual stories and situations emerge, I help the client express in therapy the pain, grief, and loss associated with them. This direct expression of the feelings connected to past painful events—the fifth stage—has the effect of reducing and possibly eliminating the compulsive need to act them out sexually. Finally, I encourage my client to talk with selected other people about what he or she has learned. If the client is married or partnered, then sharing the nonsexual stories helps the partner feel compassion, whereas the sexual behavior might have evoked only disgust or anger.

The story of my client, Jeff, is a good example of how analyzing CSS can reveal the cause of a sexual behavioral problem.

His wife, Trudy, had threatened to leave him several times. Then she filed for divorce. That's when they came to see me. Trudy told me Jeff was seeing men for sex, and Jeff didn't deny it. He had promised Trudy he would stop, but he didn't keep his promise. She was concerned that he might be gay, but she wasn't going to tolerate his behavior even if he wasn't. As is my routine in these cases, I saw Jeff in individual therapy, and he told me he was doing a lot more than Trudy realized. The easy part? He wasn't gay. The heart of the difficulty: He was a full-blown sex addict. Trudy had found out about a few of the men, but he was acting out with many more men, and he was also acting out with women. In fact, he had had hundreds of anonymous sexual encounters.

When I work with a couple where one or both individuals are having affairs, I let them know at the beginning that I have an "open secrets policy," which I learned from Janice Abrams-Spring, the author of *After the Affair: Healing the Pain and Rebuilding Trust When a Partner Has Been Unfaithful.*[4] I won't share anything one of them tells me in individual therapy that he or she wants kept confidential. If I'm working with a man such as Jeff to get to the core of his issues, then the therapeutic process won't work if he's holding back from me for fear I'll tell his wife.

I encourage sharing, but I don't enforce it. Of course, I won't keep either of their secrets if either is putting the other at risk for HIV or other STDs, or legal ramifications, or some other dangerous consequences. If nothing like that is happening, I'll keep both of their secrets.

Jeff was an extremely active sex addict, and Trudy had no idea of the extent of his activities. He used Craigslist. He used chat rooms. He used sex-contact 800 numbers. He was remarkably "successful" in setting up sexual encounters with strangers. He sometimes went to prostitutes, but he didn't like to use them. Otherwise, he wasn't particular. He liked being attractive, being admired for his looks, being seen. He sought women because he was heterosexual, but he liked men because they especially admired his body, and they weren't inclined to ask him questions. He hated it when his sex contacts asked him about himself: *Are you married? What do you do for a living? How old are you?* This questioning would completely turn him off; he would lose his erection and his state of arousal. He walked out on his sex contacts if they didn't stop asking him about himself. He wanted to be wanted, but he couldn't stand to be known.

He didn't care what sex acts they did. It wasn't the specific sex acts or specific scenes that excited him. It was all about the fact that they saw him and didn't know him. Many sex addicts have anonymous sex. That often goes with seeking out many sex partners, but the anonymity itself doesn't particularly excite them. Usually, they'll share bits and pieces about themselves with their hookups without it being a problem for them. But Jeff was phobic about it. Being known ruined the sex for him.

This "not wanting to be known" *as an erotic charge* seemed to be the key to understanding his sexual scripts, whereas his family history was the key to unlocking their nonsexual meaning. It often is, which is why I routinely do a carefully detailed family history in cases such as Jeff's. In brief, he was a product of "benign" neglect by both parents, although the cumulative effect on Jeff was anything but benign. His parents didn't have much time for him. The unstated message he received was: *We'll provide for you. We'll make sure you have food, clothing, shelter, and schooling. We'll pay for your college. But please don't tell us too much about yourself. We have other things going on in our lives. We don't have time. We're not interested.*

His parents didn't want to know him. That was painful. He eroticized this pain. The resulting sex fantasy featured anonymous sex with a partner who didn't know anything about him. The less somebody knew, and still wanted him, the bigger charge he got. He acted out sexually with both men and women, because both parents treated him the same way. So, that's what he kept reenacting with his sexual addiction; that's what he was sexualizing.

Jeff had to be treated for his sexual addiction as well as his childhood trauma. The treatment for sexual addiction includes a variety of behavior modification techniques, including twelve-step groups, just as for alcohol addiction. The psychotherapy followed the standard pattern: acknowledging what happened, feeling the powerlessness of the child, feeling a multitude of strong feelings toward the parents, and then letting out the grief, the loss, the pain, moving toward acceptance and self-comforting.

Jeff is making progress, but he's still struggling. He has yet to tell Trudy the extent of his past behavior. The focus of my work with Trudy and Jeff is to move Jeff toward healing. What he shares with her is between them. Even so, she appreciates that he is working hard at his therapy, and she's put the divorce on hold for now.

JIMMY USES HIS GOOD LOOKS TO FIND LOVE

A CSS often doesn't develop from childhood difficulties in a predictable way. In the following case, I might have guessed Jimmy's CSS would be the complete opposite of what it turned out to be.

Jimmy came to consult with me, not because his fiancée had discovered his secret life, but because he didn't want her to discover it. He wanted to give it up, but he was finding that difficult to do. He had been approached by a guy to have sex for money, and the idea of being paid meant something to Jimmy. He didn't understand why, but he was more aroused by being paid than he was by the sex. Then, he met a girl, fell in love, wondered what he was doing having sex with a man, and came to me to straighten out his life before all his hopes and dreams were destroyed by his acting out.

Jimmy was very good looking. "You ought to be on TV," people told him. "You ought to go to Hollywood." He was now thirty. He hadn't gone to Hollywood. He was a producer for a large New York advertising agency that had an office in Detroit. But his good looks had led to his current dilemma.

"I love Chrissy," he told me in his first session with me. "I make so many superficial connections in my job. Actresses. Account managers. They're in town for a project; then they're gone. Now, a beautiful, smart woman loves me. She really does. We've been dating for a year. I asked her to marry me, and she said "yes," just like that, without a moment's hesitation. For two weeks I was walking on clouds. I was in love. Someone was in love with me. Then it hit me. *Oh my God, what about Gregory?*"

"He's a photographer the agency uses sometimes. 'You are so damned good looking' was virtually the first thing he said to me. His next sentence took some of the weirdness out it. 'I do art photography as well as agency work. I'd love for you to pose for me.'"

Jimmy liked the praise, but he didn't want to get involved with Gregory. "Thanks, but no. I don't pose for people," he'd said.

But Gregory was persistent. The next time they saw each other, he said to Jimmy, "I'd pay you to pose for me. I hire models all the time. I did a show at the Ariana Gallery last year. The *Free Press* gave it a great review. You can Google it. I'd pay you more than the standard fee, because your looks are perfect. I know you said you didn't pose, but God, could I just pay you to pose once?"

"No," Jimmy insisted, "no, I don't want to do that."

Then the next week, "I hope you don't think I was coming on to you. There are guys who would pay you for *that* you know."

Jimmy still said, "no," but something tickled his imagination about being paid for sex.

Gregory picked up the thread, maybe sensing Jimmy's unspoken interest. "You look so great. I know that guys would probably pay you just to look at you, so they could jerk off and not even have sex with you."

This sex talk might have turned Jimmy off. Later, he thought it should have repulsed him. But he loved it. Gregory could tell that Jimmy was becoming more receptive.

"Well, if you ever want to get paid just to pose or whatever, I would be totally cool with anything."

Finally, they did get together. Gregory was gay, and he didn't care that Jimmy was not. In fact, it turned Gregory on that Jimmy was straight. Of course, he asked Jimmy to pose nude, but by then Jimmy expected that. As Gregory took his pictures, he spent the whole hour praising Jimmy's beautiful body. "You look so good. I've never seen a guy like you.

You're the most beautiful guy I've ever seen. You're such a man." Jimmy loved being adored, worshipped, validated, *blessed* by another man. Then, on top of all that, he got paid $400. The praise and the money together were like crack cocaine for him; something deep in his CSS was being evoked. He didn't understand this consciously, but the money carried a lot of the validation, the blessing. Because Gregory paid him, he must be worth a lot.

After the first few modeling sessions, Gregory started discreetly masturbating during the breaks, which Jimmy didn't mind. It was all part of the adoration. Later, Jimmy let Gregory suck him off. Why not? It made the guy happy. And Jimmy got $400. He'd never felt so loved in all his life.

When Jimmy came to see me, he'd fallen hard for Chrissy. She was wonderful. She turned him on. He had a future with her. Yet, he still liked getting Gregory's money and Gregory's praise.

"Do I have to tell her about Gregory?" he asked me, and I could tell he really didn't want to stop seeing Gregory. "It doesn't have anything to do with Chrissy. He mostly just jacks off while I pose."

"Before you do anything major like telling Chrissy," I suggested, "why don't we try to figure out why you feel so compelled to be with Gregory? You aren't attracted to him." I had already confirmed that Jimmy was not gay or bi. "You wouldn't be seeing him if he weren't paying you, but you don't need the money. So, what's going on?" But Jimmy had no idea.

And so we began to talk about Jimmy's family of origin. We looked at connections between his present behavior patterns and the past. "You're having this guy pay you," I told Jimmy, "and that's a big part of what turns you on. He's worshipping your manhood. Does that remind you of anything in your childhood?"

"No," Jimmy admitted. "Nobody thought I was anything special."

"What about your dad?"

"He never said anything to me. He mostly just drank beer and watched TV. Slept a lot."

"What about your mother?"

"She ran the house. Organized the chores, cooked the meals, paid the bills, made the doctor and dentist appointments, gave us rides in her car when we needed rides."

"Did your mother admire your masculinity?"

"No, I don't remember that."

"Well, what do you remember?"

Jimmy paused a long time. Finally, "I remember her making a fuss about the girls, my sisters. Their dance classes, their new dresses, all that girl stuff... Anything the girls did was a big deal."

"What about you? What about boy stuff?"

"Nah. Not really. I was in sports. She didn't seem to care."

"Did she or your father go to your games?"

"No."

"Did she or he ask you about your games? You know. *How'd it go? Did you win? What was the score?* That sort of thing?"

"No. I made Eagle Scout. I got second prize in a science fair. Nobody ever said anything about it. Mom was mostly into my sisters. When they started their periods, you'd think they'd made the honor roll. They got a boyfriend. It was a big deal. I had girlfriends. She didn't even ask their names."

"Did your father show you a little more interest than your mother?"

"No."

It didn't take too many sessions for me to recognize the pattern of Jimmy's childhood. I wanted him to see it, too. "Wow," I told him, "you really weren't valued at all, especially not as a male. Sounds like you were ignored. Your sisters were being rewarded for everything they did that was feminine, but you weren't rewarded for being masculine. You did sports, but nobody went to your games or talked about them."

"I guess so," he reluctantly agreed. "I never thought about it before."

"Eagle Scout. Science fair. Sports. And nobody said a thing about it."

He nodded. He looked sad.

He wasn't valued at home for who he was or anything he did by either parent. Nobody was criticizing him or making fun of him. They were just ignoring him. But neglect can hurt even more than abuse. Jimmy was a male, and he was specifically not being valued as a male. The girls were blessed by their mother, as girls should be. Boys need blessing by their fathers, but Jimmy didn't get that. This left him hungry for a way to become valued as a man. This need became embedded in his CSS, and later Gregory came along to fulfill it.

This family background might have led Jimmy in other directions. I've treated men whose family valued girls over boys and who compensated by being very identified with the feminine, by being cross-dressers or otherwise focused on their own feminine side. There's no formula for this, no menu to link a psychological trauma with particular adult compensations. Jimmy could have decided as a kid *all the smart money is on being feminine, so I'll be more feminine.*

Instead, he grew up starved for masculine praise. He had what we sometimes call "father hunger," which made him vulnerable to Gregory's appeal, even though Jimmy wasn't gay.

Why being paid meant so much to Jimmy I can't say. We live in a capitalist society. Money is our universal mark of approval. Or maybe we didn't uncover some nuance in Jimmy's background that would have explained it.

Jimmy's father hunger could have manifested itself in many other ways. He could have become depressed, or bitter, or suicidal. We always have to keep in mind that what a man becomes as an adult is a combination of his nature and his history, plus the butterfly effect, which is what I call random variations too complex to analyze. In the end, different people react different ways to similar childhoods. Even though we recognize and work with patterns in psychology, psychotherapy is never routine.

In any case, Jimmy was liberated enough by his therapy to be able to let go of his dependence on Gregory and marry Chrissy.

> *The Butterfly Effect*—A small "random" event of great psychological importance. The cleaning lady who picks up the crying baby, allowing him some early comfort and love that his depressed mother cannot give. The older boy who takes an interest in the little boy's hobby, giving him two fifteen-minute periods of attention that stand in for fathering for the rest of his life.

Although in therapy we tend to look at pain from childhood and early experiences, we should note one more time that positive events in a person's past can also be eroticized in the CSS. Maybe your brother spooned with you at night, because you wanted to be comforted, and now you really like to be spooned. It's erotic to you. Well, nothing is wrong with that. Not all CSS come from painful experiences.

SUMMARY OF THE CSS THERAPY PROCESS

The issue is how to gain mastery over a troublesome sexual behavior. In the course of therapy I look for psychological trauma and other root causes such as negative influencing, early sexual experiences, difficult sexual experiences, social influences, and other significant factors. I use an exploration of CSS as a doorway to discover the root causes of the behavior.

Therapy proceeds in six stages: (1) clarifying the troubling sexual behavior or interests; (2) getting the details of the CSS; (3) getting a family and social history; (4) connecting the CSS to nonsexual narratives; (5) expressing in therapy the pain, grief, and loss associated with these narratives, reducing and possibly eliminating the compulsive need to act them out sexually; and (6) selectively sharing what has been learned with others, especially the partner.

In the majority of the cases I have treated, this therapeutic process has given the client greater mastery and choice over his or her behavior, the partner greater understanding and empathy, and the couple a better chance at making their relationship functional and life affirming.

* * *

In this chapter, we have looked at the deep psychological mechanisms that unconsciously control our behavior and how therapy deals with them. Next, we take a higher-level view of sexual behavior patterns that look gay but are not. When is kinky sex just kinky sex and when is it a serious psychological problem?

12

ARE YOU WHAT YOU ORGASM?

Kinks That "Look Gay"

If you go to war with your sexuality, you will lose, and end up in more trouble than before you started. I have never seen a single exception to this principle.

—Jack Morin[1]

This book has been written to help a wife concerned that her husband might be gay or bisexual. She may be worried that he has a secret sex life, or that he is "coming out" and will leave her when he realizes that he is gay. She may have found evidence that she believes suggests he's gay—for example, porn sites that he likes. However, some sexual behaviors thought to be only for gay men are also engaged in by straight men. In fact, some of these behaviors are engaged in *only* by straight men.

Of course, a sexual behavior may be of concern in and of itself, whether or not it is "gay," and later we'll consider some reasons to be concerned.

We're using "kink," as before, as a nontechnical term to refer to any atypical sexual interest or behavior.

We've already seen in part I different situations in which straight men seem to be gay. Tom, in chapters 1 and 2, had sex with men, acting out the homosexual behavioral imprinting of the sexual abuse he suffered as a child from his coach. Joel (chapter 3) and Adam (chapter 5) have kinks that look gay but don't really involve sex with men. We might take David (chapter 4), who is into anal sex, as another example of "looking gay" but being straight. In this chapter, we'll consider some more examples. Also, we'll summarize and extend the various facts about kinks we've presented in part I.

EDDIE'S KINK

Eddie came to see me because his girlfriend, Amber, caught him looking at "shemale" porn. She thought he might be gay and told him to get help or get out.

"I like chicks with dicks," he said to me. He grinned, but it was to cover his embarrassment. He had obviously rehearsed that line so he could tell me quickly and get it over with. I was glad he was willing to talk about his problem right away. With my clients who struggle with sexual issues, I try to get them to talk about their fantasies and behaviors as soon as they are comfortable with it, although I always take things slowly if that's what they need.

"It looks to me like you're feeling ashamed about your sexual interests," I said. "Am I right about that?"

"Very!" he responded. "I just want to be normal. When I met Amber, I felt normal. Boy meets girl. Boy is turned on by girl. What could be more normal than that?"

"Can I ask you to tell me about 'chicks with dicks?'" I asked.

"I never thought about shemales until I saw some shemale porn," Eddie said, "but then it hit me like a ton of bricks. I was right into it. I couldn't stop going to those sites. It bothered me when I thought about it, it was so weird, but shemales turn me on. No question."

"Do you have a specific special fantasy? Something that turns you on the most?"

"I don't know," he said. "I just like to imagine I'm with a beautiful sexy woman who happens to have a dick. She's hot, but she's got a cock. We're holding each other tightly. I'm kissing her, feeling her tits against me and her cock rubbing up and down on my body, and then I'm sucking her off. I look up and see her beautiful face and boobs."

I went through my checklist—the beach test, youthful noticing, and the rest. I asked Eddie if he ever had a sexual attraction to other men. Would he ever want to be sucking someone off and look up and see a guy instead of a beautiful woman? He said "no," and he wasn't ambiguous about it. He did not want to look up and see a masculine man or an effeminate man or any kind of man. It had to be a woman from the waist up. We went over these aspects for several sessions.

"You're not gay," I finally told him. "And you're not bi either. Gay men are attracted to men."

"See," Eddie said, "that's the point. Amber says I have to be gay. What she says is, 'Shemales have penises, so they're men. I'm turned on by shemales, so I'm turned on by men, so that means I'm gay.' That sounds pretty right to me."

"I understand," I said, "but sexual interests are not logical like that, and sexual orientation is much more complicated. Gay men are attracted to men who look like men. Put bluntly, they don't want to be sucking dick and look up to see a woman."

I told him in my thirty years as a therapist and sexologist, I've seen many straight men "into" pre-op transwomen, but never once has a gay man come to see me about this fantasy. "All those thousands of porn sites," I told him, "they're for straight men. Gay guys have zero interest in this."

"If I'm not gay, am I bi?"

"Speaking generally, you could like this kind of porn and be bi, but in your case I don't see any signs that you are significantly bi. I also want to assure you, nothing is inherently pathological about being turned on by these fantasies."

I explained to him about sexual kinks and how a lot of straight men's kinks are mistaken for gayness.

"Interest in pre-op transwomen might seem obviously gay," I told him, "but this has been studied repeatedly, and I've confirmed it in my practice. Gay men are never drawn to transwomen as a sexual kink, and lots of straight men are."

Transwomen, Pre-op and Post-op—Some men and women know they are a gender different from what their bodies indicate. That is, a person may have the body of a man but know she is a woman or have the body of a woman but know he is a man. People who know they were "born into the wrong body" can be assisted medically and hormonally to modify their bodies to transition to the gender they identify with. A pre-op transwoman is a person born with a male's body who has undergone hormonal treatments so that she has body features of a woman, including womanly breasts, but has not undergone surgery to convert her penis into a vagina. A post-op transwoman has, in addition, undergone this bottom surgery. I need to emphasize here that the sexual kink/fantasy/interest some men have about transwomen has nothing to do with how a typical transwoman sees herself, what she wants from relationships, or how she wants to be in the world.

Men Sexually Interested in Transwomen (MSTW)—Some men are especially attracted to pre-op transwomen. Following sexologists Martin S. Weinber and Colin J. Williams,[*] I will refer to such men as "men sexually interested in transwomen," MSTW being their acronym. I see in my practice many MSTW. Often, they come to see me concerned that they might be gay.

[*]Martin S. Weinber and Colin J. Williams, "Men Sexually Interested in Transwomen (MSTW): Gendered Embodiment and the Construction of Sexual Desire," *Journal of Sex Research, 47*(4) (2009): 374–83.

Let's pause to note an important point: A man might fall in love with a transgender woman, pre-op or post-op, and that's a matter of the human heart as well as human sexuality. It has nothing to do with what we are talking about here. We're talking here about kinks and objectification for erotic stimulation; that is, sexual obsessions and fantasies, not love or relationships. I am also not judging whether one is better or worse. I am simply pointing out the differences.

What makes an MSTW? There are theories, but no "proof." Freud refers to a belief by a young boy that his mother once had a penis but lost it (Google "Freud, castration anxiety"). Naturally, if a child did have such ideas at an early age, we can imagine a residual MSTW kink developing under some circumstances.

Other theories for how MSTW are made include (1) the erotic appeal of gender fluidity, in that aspects of both genders appear; (2) a biological randomness in how sexual interests get established—for example, in utero hormonal influences are sometimes associated with gender dysphoria; why not MSTW also?; (3) a heterosexual man with an extreme fear of women might settle on the MSTW kink to resolve the tension between his sexuality and his fear; (4) a man might be drawn to homoerotic fantasies but homophobia forces him into the MSTW "compromise." (5) Finally, there is a theme (as found in some religions) of an interest in multi-sexed people who combine masculine and feminine characteristics.

We do not know where the MSTW kink comes from, but we do know it has nothing to do with being gay. Ogi Ogas and Sai Gaddam in *A Billion Wicked Thoughts: What the Internet Tells Us about Sexual Relationships*[2] describe their research on transsexual porn. They cite a blog by transsexual performer Wendy Williams in which she writes, "Transexual Porn is classified as Straight Specialty," and the authors go on to say that research shows this porn is viewed primarily by straight and bisexual men.

TYLER'S CROSS-DRESSING

Tyler was a forty-year-old man who came to see me because his wife, Lisa, was divorcing him. She had found a video he'd made of himself masturbating and wearing women's clothes, high heels, a wig, and make-up. Lisa was horrified.

She looked and found a number of similar videos. She went through his things and found the women's clothes and the shoes. She also found matches from a local gay bar and magazines of local gay hot spots.

She stacked all of this on their bed, put one of the videos on the screen of their computer running in a continuous loop, took the kids, and went to stay with her mother. Tyler came home, saw what she had done, and was mortified.

He told me his wife didn't want to talk with him about anything but divorce. She was convinced he was gay, and nothing he could say would convince her otherwise.

The truth is that gay men do not wear women's clothing for sexual arousal. When gay men dress up like women, it is for performance. Impersonating a woman can be funny or skillful, but gay men do not become sexually aroused by doing "drag." They just enjoy the campy fun of it and the art of the performance.

It didn't surprise me that Lisa would think Tyler was gay after finding the cross-dressing videos and the gay paraphernalia, but I knew what was happening, because I have seen this dozens of times before in my office.

Men who cross-dress are almost always straight or bisexual. They have an obligatory desire—a compulsion, or at least a strong impulse—to dress as women, and they get a sexual release from it. Often, these men have been cross-dressing since childhood. They report to me that they used to put on their mothers' underwear; cross-dressing excited them even as children.

Gay little boys often report wearing their mother's clothes, too, but they don't experience sexual excitement. Instead, they do this to identify with females, because there are so few gay male role models they can identify with or have permission to admire. I expect that gay boys and teens will give up using female role models in the future as more and more gay males become publicly prominent and gay masculinity is available for these gay boys to emulate.

The fact that Tyler went to gay bars did not surprise me, nor did it indicate that he was gay. Many straight and bi men who cross-dress eventually want to go out in public. They want to be seen as, and treated like, women. Gay clubs and bars are safe places where they can do this.

I remember being surprised when I first met and spoke to a cross-dressing man at a gay bar who said he was straight. At first I didn't believe him. He told me he was not at risk there of being beaten or humiliated for cross-dressing. He admitted that some gay men hassled him, but nothing like he would have experienced at a straight bar.

Sometimes, a cross-dresser wants to be kissed and hugged by a man, or even be sexual or romantic. The cross-dresser doesn't want to be a woman. He is aroused by feeling like one. His behavior looks and sounds gay, but it isn't. Gay men feel and know they are men and want that reinforced. They don't want to be seen as female or experience life as a woman. When a gay man does drag, he is presenting as a woman, but he isn't sexually aroused by it.

Certain forms of BDSM play and cuckolding and other similar turn-ons in the realm of dominance and submission involve humiliating a man by feminizing him. Straight, bi, and gay men may dress as women to help them feel more humiliated in a sexual scene, which is completely different from the cross-dressing kink we are considering here.

Tyler would have enjoyed cross-dressing with his wife, but she wanted no part of it. In fact, early in their marriage Tyler had hinted that it might be fun in the bedroom for him to wear her panties and bra, but she was completely repulsed by the idea.

Lisa's response is a common one. Many women are strongly turned off by the idea of effeminate men. This is unfortunate, because usually cross-dressing men are quite masculine in every other aspect of their lives. *My Husband Betty*[3] describes a heterosexual couple who have comfortably adapted to the husband's cross-dressing.

Robert Stoller, author of *Perversion*,[4] has written extensively on cross-dressing. He theorizes that it might be a natural way for a straight man to embrace his feminine side, because our culture doesn't allow any other such outlets.

Tyler was depressed and distraught over Lisa's reaction. He desperately wanted to avoid a divorce. He loved his wife; he didn't want to be separated from his children. He promised her he would stop cross-dressing. He threw out all the clothes and deleted all the videos. However, I knew this would not last for long. Kinks such as these are very strong; and the more a person fights them, the stronger they become. The best way to deal with them is to accept and manage the acting out. The compulsion can diminish with acceptance and shame reduction, but the impulse will most likely not go away completely, even after therapy.

Lisa could not tolerate Tyler's kink at all. Although she eventually came to understand that he was not gay, the image of him dressed as a women disgusted her so much that she couldn't get over it. She insisted on the divorce.

ARE YOU WHAT YOU ORGASM?

It's a trick question, because the answer is "yes and no." What turns you on is a strong signifier of who you are and what you've experienced. That was the main point of the previous chapter on core sexual scripts. On the other hand, what turns you on does not determine your sexual identity in any simpleminded way. We've seen this illustrated in the cases of David from chapter 4 and George in chapter 11, who like gay porn but are straight.

Here's another illustration of the disconnect between porn and identity. Many people might guess that lesbians would be turned off by gay male pornography. However, "Hot Man on Man Action (And the Lesbians Who Love Watching It)"[5] makes the point that that's not always the case. The author presents some ideas on why this type of porn might be generally engaging: The actors are all very hot, and the focus is on the sex; anal sex is erotic; the actors can't fake arousal, so what the viewer sees is real; and, finally, most gay male porn is just more "down and dirty" than most lesbian erotica.

Your preference in porn doesn't define your sexual orientation.

Another reason why someone who is not gay or bisexual might be attracted to gay male pornography is that the actors are usually engaged in a mutual, reciprocal, and power-balanced sex act in which no one is being objectified in a humiliating or demeaning way, and both actors seem to want the other to enjoy the sex. This is unlike much of straight porn, where the male is usually dominant and the woman is submissive. She is there only to please him. Again, we see that the nuances of sexual interest can be important and are missed in simpleminded interpretations.

WHEN IS A KINK A PROBLEM?

In keeping with using "kink" to mean any atypical sexual interest or behavior, let's call the person with the kink a "kinkster." For a person to qualify as a kinkster, he needs to have more than just a passing mild interest in the kink but rather long-term intense urges, fantasies, or behaviors involving the kink. I will often refer in this section to kinksters as "he," because this book is mainly about male sexual behaviors and interests, and many more men than women are kinksters. The ratio 20:1 is often mentioned.[6]

A kinkster may be having trouble or causing trouble with his kink. Only then does the kinkster have a psychological disorder that might call for a psychological (or legal) intervention. The "trouble" might be compulsive behaviors, or problems in the kinkster's relationships, or conflicts for the kinkster with his own values and beliefs. If the kinkster is causing harm—for example, if the kink were pedophilia, or if the kinkster were having compulsive unprotected sex with many partners—then the kinkster's disorder would definitely require an intervention.

If the kinkster's trouble with a kink is mainly the shame of it, then therapy can help lift the weight of the shame. Such shame is often culturally induced. Once the kinkster accepts his kink and no longer buys into society's negative judgment about it, then the problem often goes away. The problem was the shame, not the kink.

There are three recognized levels of attachment of a kinkster to his kink. First, a person may enjoy a kink but doesn't need it to get aroused. It's completely optional. Second, a person may prefer a specific kink but sometimes engages in sex without it. And, third, the kinkster may need the kink to become aroused.

Let me note that kinks are often associated with compulsive sexual behavior. The kinkster is wasting too much time and money on the kink, he wants to stop but can't, and he is harming himself or others. In this case, strong measures must be taken to free the kinkster of his compulsion, and sometimes permanent abstinence is the only way to recover control over his life. In other cases, I've treated kinksters who could indulge in their kinks in a controlled way after treatment and manage their lives with this outlet. Both situations arise; no hard-and-fast rule exists about how kinks must be managed.

Lots of men have kinks. A man might be extremely turned on by a specific type of object or a body part—separate from the rest of the body—or a very specific scripted fantasy or situation. Eddie's interest in transwomen is not really an interest in a type of person he'd like to have a relationship with. His interest is a kink. It's a fantasy. Only a fantasy. Many women I talk with simply can't believe the weird kinds of kinks their men have.

I had a client once who liked watching a video of a penis being jacked off. He wasn't gay. He was imagining that penis going inside his wife. But the body part was enough. That's rarely the case for a woman. She's not going to look at a penis and be turned on. She wants the whole man. (We look further at this difference between the fantasies of men and women in chapter 14.)

If I am trying to help someone who is bothered by an otherwise harmless kink, then my therapy does not focus on eliminating the kink. Research shows that kinks are often permanently embedded in the client's core sexual scripts and cannot be "eliminated." What is possible is to add to someone's sexual fantasies and behaviors so they are not so dependent on the kink for arousal. In other words, rather than coaching a client to remove something, I help him include new things in addition to his kink that can arouse and excite him.

Many who possess a kink find it disturbing, time-consuming, and intrusive; and they don't want this particular desire and interest to be so compelling. They will ask me if they have a sexual addiction. That diagnosis can be difficult to make, even for therapists. What we look for to diagnose sexual addiction is that the kinkster's behavior should be strongly interfering with his or her ability to connect with people and form relationships; it should also be getting in the way of employment or school or other tasks of daily living. A nonaddictive kink can be incorporated into a person's sexual life and not interfere with daily routine. If the reported distress derives mainly from shame, then I treat the shame but don't attempt to "eliminate" the kink. For more on sexual addiction, see the website of the Society for the Advancement of Sexual Health, www.sash.net.

Kinks—A person (usually a man) might need to focus on a specific object or body part or scripted sexual fantasy to become aroused. We say the person "has a kink" for the object, part, or fantasy, and call the person a kinkster. I use the informal "kink" as a catchall term for a range of more technical and specific terms. (See the disclaimer in the front of this book.) People commonly use the term "fetish" as we are using "kink," although the clinical definition of fetish is more specific.

PARAPHILIAS

The word "paraphilia" was coined by a psychiatrist, Wilhelm Stekel, in the 1920s to replace the more pejorative "perversion." The most current psychological definition of paraphilia, as given in the American Psychiatric Association's *Diagnostic and Statistical Manual of Mental Disorders, 5th Edition*, published in 2013 and commonly called the *DSM-5*, defines a paraphilia as an "atypical sexual practice." That is, a paraphilia is exactly what we've been calling a kink.

The *DSM-5* goes on to define a "paraphilic disorder" as a paraphilia that includes distress or impairment in functioning, or that inherently involves non-consenting individuals. A happy kinkster who isn't causing anyone harm has a paraphilia but not a paraphilic disorder. He doesn't require any kind of medical or psychological treatment.

Previously, the word "paraphilia" was defined to mean what is now meant by a paraphilic disorder (as in the *DSM-4*). Therefore, if a therapist is using the word "paraphilia," you will want to check which meaning, the old or the new, he or she is intending.

It is a matter of debate among professionals when a paraphilia should be classified as a paraphilic disorder. The practical distinction is the amount of impairment the person with the paraphilia is experiencing in his or her life because of the paraphilia, or the amount of harm he or she is causing others because of it, rather than the nature of the paraphilia itself. Research on the issue of when paraphilias become disorders is ongoing.

Accepted scientific research has not established an explanation for why many more men than women have paraphilias, although some hints have come from prenatal neurological development.[7] In fact, the reasons paraphilias develop in the first place is not well understood.[8]

* * *

One possible reason a man's behaviors might seem gay is that he is gay. In the next chapter, we consider the gay husband, and how a mixed-orientation marriage might be managed successfully.

13

YOUR MAN IS GAY OR BISEXUAL

Now What?

Yet if Josh and Lolly Weed have become the LDS' best-known "mixed-orientation marriage," the stories of other couples in similar circumstances show there is no single answer for every situation.

—Peggy Fletcher Stack[1]

DO YOU HAVE TO GET DIVORCED?

No, you do not. More than two-thirds of mixed-orientation marriages, where one spouse is straight and the other gay, end in divorce, but divorce is not inevitable.

A couple always has options, and this chapter is about options and choices for a mixed-orientation couple. I'll include some comments at the end of this chapter on the case where your man is bisexual.

AFTER THE STORM: OPTIONS

For some time, you may feel betrayed, angry, and sad, as discussed in chapter 10, but you will get past that, and then you'll want to consider your options. Basically, you and your man have two options, and losses are associated with each. You need to discuss what you want to keep and what you're willing to give up. The two options are:

1. Divorce and go your separate ways. Your man may choose to be very "out" as a gay man or not, depending on many personal factors. If you have children, coparenting will be the best option for them.
2. The second option is to stay married, allow him some mutually agreed upon "gay outlets," share your "secret" with a few selected friends and family members, and live in your community as a heterosexual couple.

I have supported couples choosing both of these options. No one has a right to tell you that you have to divorce. After all, it's your marriage, and a loving partner is worth fighting for, even fighting conventional "wisdom" and social pressure.

My advice is for the two of you to talk together and consider everything about your relationship. You might consider that you have every reason to love and trust this man, that you can believe him if he says he wants to work to keep you and your family. The man might consider whether he really needs to have sex with men. He might be able to claim his identity by meeting occasionally with gay men, staying in touch on Facebook, and letting his gay friends know that he wants to remain sexually faithful to his wife.

I realize that other possible options exist, but the two I've named above are by far the most common and the most pragmatic. Yes, a few couples have tried to remain married and be completely "out," but mixed-orientation miscegenation is as taboo today as black-white miscegenation was fifty years ago. Both straight and gay communities put enormous pressure on the man and woman in a mixed-orientation marriage, and few marriages can stand up under this social, family, and religious pressure.

Another "option" is for the gay man to live his own secret gay life and keep his wife completely in the dark. Naturally, homophobia has led to this miserable arrangement many times in the past and still does today. It is described in the best seller *On the Down Low*.[2] We can hardly view this as any kind of choice for an enlightened couple, and I won't discuss it further in this book.

Some couples try to "live straight" and imagine that they will be able to not acknowledge the husband's gayness in any way. Generally, a gay man will feel a lot of emotional distress, grief, and depression if he is living so deeply in the closet. This will happen even if, or maybe I should say especially if, he is in denial about his gayness.

Sometimes a wife comes to me. "Oh, my god. I think my husband has been gay all along. With his family and friends being so homophobic, he never could have told me." I have to advise wives whose husbands are members of an especially homophobic subculture or religion to be aware of the difficulty he will have in talking to her about his sexuality. And, of course, the danger is that he is living a part of his life in secret, not telling her.

A number of books are directed toward straight spouses of gay partners; for example, Amity Pierce Buxton's *The Other Side of the Closet: The Coming-Out Crisis for Straight Spouses and Families*[3] and Grever and Bowman's *When Your Spouse Comes Out: A Straight Mate's Recovery Manual.*[4] I also recommend the Straight Spouse Network (www.straightspouse.org).

I always urge a couple at least to be clear with each other about their sexual and identity issues and to seek the assistance of a therapist, if necessary.

THREE TRUTHS

First, if your husband says he didn't know he was gay when he married you, he probably didn't know. He most likely interpreted his gay interests as sexual "kinks," and he convinced himself they would fade away after he married. Most of my male clients who are gay and married to women didn't know they were gay when they married. They often don't know they're gay when they first come to see me. Typically they are homophobic and want me to reassure them and their wives that they aren't gay. I've heard more than once, "I'm not gay. I just like to have sex with men." These gay men identify their behavior as "only sexual." They are in denial about its deeper meaning for themselves.

Second, if your husband says he loves you, he most likely does. A gay man can truly love a woman, have satisfying and regular sex with her, and want to stay married to her while being uninterested in other women sexually. Thus, love can conquer (but not change) orientation. That is, the man is still gay, and he loves you.

> *Love Conquers Orientation*—A gay man can fall in love with a woman. Even so, he is still gay.

Third, most couples don't talk about sex and their expectations for each other in a marriage, but you can do it. (I offer specific guidelines in the next two chapters.) The ideal here is for the two of you to learn to talk honestly with each other about your sexual needs, and other needs, and what to do about them. You may fear that because he is gay, he will leave you. He may fear that if he admits he is gay, you will leave him. An agreement not to bolt may be very helpful.

HOW DO YOU MANAGE A MIXED-ORIENTATION MARRIAGE?

A marriage doesn't have to have a label, just as a person doesn't have to have a label. Lots of people do lots of different things, and often what they do doesn't fit into a tidy category. Nobody should ever tell anybody else what should or shouldn't be going on in their own particular marriage. But, of course, people do.

Anyway, it's not about "marriage." It's about the people in the marriage. Get rid of your rigid definition of marriage and develop your own ideas about what you want *your* marriage to look like.

How much accommodation will you have to make to the man's gayness? Not all gay husbands need to have sex with other men; sometimes, outlets that don't involve sexual contact are possible. However, some couples allow a certain amount of sexual openness for the man, and also for the woman.

Two categories of accommodations need to be considered:

1. Social accommodations: One extreme is to tell almost nobody. In the other extreme, the gay husband is allowed a gay social life. The couple doesn't make a point of being "out," but their closest friends and relatives know. The wife might even socialize with his gay friends, but probably they don't socialize as a mixed-orientation

couple with straight friends, religious organizations, work-related gatherings, school, and so forth.

2. Accommodations of gay identity: One extreme is for him to do almost no homosocializing, perhaps a little contact over the Internet, never in person. Other men want to gather occasionally with gay men, perhaps for gay community events, but are capable of avoiding sexual contacts. Still others feel they need to have an anonymous hookup every once in a while, but they never want to know the guy and they're completely disinclined to be emotionally involved with men. Other "open-marriage" arrangements are possible.

I have counseled mixed-orientation couples where all varieties of these types of adaptations have been mutually acceptable and have worked to allow the marriage to be stable and successful.

MIXED-ORIENTATION MARRIAGES ARE MORE TABOO THAN GAY MARRIAGES

Perhaps you thought that wherever gayness was accepted, mixed-orientation marriages would be accepted. That's not the case.

The statistic that more than two-thirds of mixed-orientation marriages end in divorce is frequently cited to "prove" that mixed-orientation marriages are inherently unstable or "unnatural." Considering the amount of pressure put on the individuals in a mixed-orientation marriage, it's remarkable that so many find a way to thrive. Gay friends will work on the man. The woman's friends and family, and even therapists, will work on her. The wife is flooded with negative comments: "He will leave you" and "Don't you care that you're not his only one?" Gay men can be even more critical than straight people toward the gay guy.

Prejudiced people are certain something is *wrong* about what the couple is doing. It's somehow disloyal to both the tribe of straight people and the tribe of gays. We're talking here about a prejudice that is no less strong than the old taboo against interracial marriage.

This blind and rabid prejudice is the reason that I counsel discretion for mixed-orientation couples. If the couple decides to stay together, then they can share their "secret" with each other and maybe a few selected friends, but they cannot expect to be "out" to the world. Not yet. Typically, they cannot be out to their families, to their religious communities, or at work. They most likely can't be out to their younger children, because they can't be out at school.

All this prejudice against mixed-orientation couples is particularly ironic, because for many women, a gay man might make a fine husband. The fact that a man is more turned on by men than women simply may not be the most important factor for her or for him. I have had women report to me that they favor gay male partners, because the men tend to be less patriarchal and more appreciative of women than are straight men.

We keep coming back to the idea of individual choices. No "marriage template" fits everyone. Each marriage is two individuals wanting to connect in a way that makes sense to them as individuals. Mixed-orientation marriages abound, and they may be the best possible marriages for the individuals involved. We don't usually hear about them, because prejudice forces secrecy.

> *Prejudice Forces Secrecy*—We don't hear about most successful mixed-orientation marriages, and "scientific" surveys don't necessarily reflect accurate data.

KEEPING SECRETS

The mixed-orientation couple (mostly) will have to keep the gay aspect of their identity secret, and this "keeping secrets" will weigh heavily on the relationship, whether or not the individuals are conscious of it. Imagine a straight couple not being able to tell everybody that they're married, that they love each other. It would weigh on them. In keeping secrets, the couple is *managing* what people know of them, their image, their profile. They're not showing who they really are. Thus, the issue of "secrets" becomes central to maintaining the marriage. Some people keep secrets easily; other people don't. But let's be clear. A secret about identity is particularly psychologically difficult to keep. Something deep in the human psyche wants to proclaim allegiance to its group, to claim pride and membership with kindred people.

Individuals differ on how heavily it would weigh on them to keep an important secret. Suppose you're a secret mixed-orientation couple; and suppose you're out with other couples, and they're making gay jokes. Because you're "in hiding," you may be inhibited from objecting, because you don't want to draw attention to yourself by identifying too closely with gay causes.

I told one gay couple I was counseling, in this case two men, "You're a couple. You might or might not tell your mothers that your boyfriend is your boyfriend. You may always refer to him only as a friend. You may have a 100 percent good reason for doing that. And maybe you're not 'out' at work, so you never bring him to an office party, and it makes total sense. But keeping this secret still has negative effects on your relationship. You have to be aware of that. This suppression of an important part of who you are may push you toward depression, bitterness, or other forms of lonely grief, both as a couple and as individuals."

Being a secret mixed-orientation couple may not be as burdensome as being a secret gay couple. After all, you're out socially as a married couple. What you're not out about is, let's say, that the man has gay outlets. In some ways that's an easier secret; we're often private about our sex lives anyway. It may not be as burdensome as being gay and in the closet, but it will be a burden. It's not only a sexual secret. It's an identity secret, not just of the man, but of the couple, too.

In the background, the dark shadow of unequal treatment under the law lies across all secret mixed-orientation marriages with children. In Nazi Germany, some women were married to secretly Jewish men. One word from her to the Gestapo would destroy him. Only a saint could manage this kind of power differential and still have a sane and fair marital relationship. This isn't the exaggeration it might seem. Many judges still habitually award sole custody of the children to women divorcing gay men, giving her the power to separate him from his children forever.

ACKNOWLEDGING IDENTITY IN A MIXED-ORIENTATION MARRIAGE

A gay or bisexual orientation is not a sexual preference. It is an identity. My bottom-line rule for a gay or bisexual man, whether or not he is in a mixed-orientation marriage, is that he needs to acknowledge his identity. How an individual does this "acknowledging" varies depending on a number of factors, but what this means to most of the gay men I've counseled is some level of homosocializing. That may include sex, but it may not. The socializing might be limited to Internet interactions.

In any case, if a gay man is denied his need to gather with people like him and to affirm his identity, he will have to deal with grief, bitterness, and depression for the rest of his life. Homophobia may limit how "out" a gay man will choose to be, but my gay clients who do not find positive ways to affirm their identities tend to have severe psychological problems. On the other hand, it is my experience that bisexual men mostly into women don't need a lot of socializing with other bi or gay men.

The big question is: How can a gay man affirm his identity with other gay men and at the same time remain true to you, his wife? Will the two of you agree that he must remain traditionally faithful; or will you have a more open marriage, and if so, under what mutually agreed-upon rules?

Now is a time for questions and negotiations. What exactly does he need? What do you need? Staying together could still offer many benefits for both of you if you can find common ground. I think that honesty and transparency are the only absolute requirements. Whatever he does, he should have your informed consent.

> *Homosocializing*—Gay people connecting with each other to affirm their gay identities.

One point should be made about "open marriages. Some people think that if you open up your relationship, it's the beginning of the end. That's not necessarily true. Sometimes people "open" a failing marriage as a last-ditch effort to save it. The divorce that follows is not a result of opening the marriage but rather all that came before. *The Ethical Slut: A Guide to Infinite Sexual Possibilities*[5] and *Opening Up: A Guide to Creating and Sustaining Open Relationships*[6] discuss consensual non-monogamy as a lifestyle and provide practical guidance on how such long-term relationships work and are put into practice.

In any marriage, nobody knows what will happen years down the line. For gay husbands, people foolishly and falsely "know" the only way the marriage can go: He will have sex with men, fall in love with a man, and leave you. The truth is that his love for you and his family may motivate him to satisfy his identity needs in a variety of ways. I have seen many stable mixed marriages. One couple I counseled twenty years ago are still together. Many straight marriages do not survive twenty years. Marriage has no guarantees. Every case has to live on its own merits.

THE BISEXUAL HUSBAND

Bisexuality is complicated, because it exists in so many variations. Universal agreement is almost impossible, even among bisexuals, on what a bisexual is and isn't. Some people still argue that there are no bisexuals. Others insist that everybody is bisexual. Some people call themselves bisexual while having relationships with individuals of only one gender; others have sex with both genders but insist they are either straight or gay. Advocates of "sexual fluidity" claim that labels such as "bisexual" (and "gay" and "straight") may not always be useful or meaningful.

If you are a woman connected to a man who thinks he might be bisexual, then you can't make any assumptions. You have to talk with him about what he means and what he wants. Ask him about his needs as a bisexual. Then you both can move on to a mutual understanding of what "rules" your relationship will operate under. One myth is that bisexuals cannot be faithfully monogamous, because of their strong draw to both men and women, but individuals differ. A woman wanting a relationship with a bisexual man should discuss frankly what she's expecting and listen to what he's expecting. Although a bisexual man has a "gay side" that needs to be acknowledged, sometimes mere "acknowledgment" is all he needs.

In theory, because the man is not gay, that is, he is sexually attracted to women as well as men, it is less likely he will fall in love with a man and feel an overwhelming urge to leave his heterosexual marriage for his new love. But the truth is that people leave their marriages all the time for a new, better, more exciting, or "whatever" lover. Making generalizations is foolish and misleading. You have to talk with your man. You have to negotiate. You have to make agreements. You have to hope for the best.

One type of bisexual husband who has come to me for counseling quite a bit is what I call "hetero-emotional homosexual." Basically, this man is very committed to his woman but feels drawn to have sexual relations with men "on the side." In chapter 7, we met Sam and Jillian. He was totally committed to his marriage and to being honest with Jillian, and he wanted to negotiate with her for permission for him to have purely sexual (that is, not emotional) relations with men from time to time.

A typical story I have seen begins with the man entering my office with his wife and not identifying himself as bisexual. He may be aware that he has some sexual attraction toward men and he may even have acted on that attraction, but he doesn't consider that a significant part of who he is. He married his wife because he fell in love with her and he wanted a family. And he's happy with that for a while, perhaps even for decades, and then, because he has suppressed his bisexuality, he finds himself having sex with men. His psyche is saying, *Hey, you're bi. You're bi. I want you to realize that. Remember me?*

Now he comes to therapy with his wife, often because he has been caught having affairs, although some men have come to see me by themselves, because they are upset with their compulsive sexual behavior and want to understand it. So then (after a course of therapy) I tell him, "It looks like you're bisexual. You always were. You didn't know, but this part of you is trying to express itself." Often, in my experience, once he has recognized and acknowledged his bisexuality, he doesn't need to have sex on the side with men anymore. If he is truly bi and not gay, then his wife may well be enough for him.

The deep complexities of bisexuality were given a very complete treatment by Fritz Klein in his classic *The Bisexual Option*.[7] This is still a go-to source for basic ideas on the concept of bisexuality. *Dual Attraction: Understanding Bisexuality*[8] is also a good reference, and the *New York Times* article "The Scientific Quest to Prove—Once and for All—That Someone Can Be Truly Attracted to Both a Man and a Woman: Bisexuality Comes Out of the Closet" summarizes much current thinking.[9] Useful information can be found at bisexual.org, a joint project of The American Institute of Bisexuality and the Bisexual Foundation.

LOVE CAN KEEP YOU TOGETHER

The easiest option is to break up. Then everyone can stay in a category, and nobody is made uncomfortable because the rules of social prejudice are being challenged.

Maintaining a mixed-orientation marriage requires enduring the stress of keeping some secrets and being discreet about identity. The individuals in the couple need to have their eyes open about that. The more liberal the community they live in, the better, but even the most liberal community may be bigoted about mixed-orientation couples. The couple may need to be in therapy to deal with the stress.

Despite the dangers and difficulties, I still urge couples to consider staying together, to preserve the love that brought them together in the first place. It takes a lot of work, but you can do it. Your lives don't have to be dictated so that everybody around you will be maximally comfortable. Let them be uncomfortable. It will do them good.

* * *

Can you get into trouble talking with your partner about what turns him on? Absolutely! We consider the ins and outs of this in the next chapter.

14

SEX FANTASIES AND SEX TALK

How Much Do You Need to Know?

Men and women are often sexually stimulated by different things. . . .
Men . . . are sexually turned on by visual stimuli. Even when men
fantasize, they conjure up vivid images of body parts and copulations.

—Helen Fisher[1]

Chapter 15 will show you how to create a written agreement about
sexual boundaries. This agreement will serve as a clear understanding of
what sexual behavior is allowed, what is forbidden, and (in a more playful spirit) what you'd like to try. Chapter 14 is preliminary to chapter 15.
Here, we consider what to talk about, what not to talk about, and how to
think about and explore sexual fantasies and interests.

For simplicity, I am writing the chapter from the point of view of a
woman married to a man who is straight. Most of what is here would
apply if he were gay.

Your man has been in some kind of sexual trouble, and because of
that, he especially needs to understand his sexual self. He should know
what his core sexual scripts are, and what they are connected to in his
past. The details are important for him, and often he will need a therapist
to clarify and understand them. This was the main theme of chapters 11
and 12. But you, his wife, usually don't need to know the details of his
fantasies. In fact, it is often better if you don't.

A couple needs an agreement about the boundaries of their sexual *behavior*, which is the theme of the next chapter. On the other hand, they do not need to set boundaries on thoughts and fantasies. In fact, I advise couples to be careful about even talking about the details of their sexual fantasies. Sometimes, of course, sharing fantasies can be useful or helpful or fun. I offer guidelines in the second half of this chapter for the wife who wishes to explore the alien world of male sexual fantasies. But I advise caution, especially for a woman who doesn't know what she's getting into. Why the need for caution?

First, sexual fantasies can include disturbing elements. I believe the content of fantasies is no more real than the content of dreams. A person may fantasize about things he or she would never do. Still, a sexual fantasy might be disturbing to hear about if it involves violence or "perversions" or other "disgusting" elements. I've had women in my office, in reaction to their men's fantasies, say something like, "How could he want to do that to somebody or want somebody to do that to him?" Or even, "You can't be in my house if you have those thoughts in your head." One of my female clients told me that she couldn't have sex with her husband after she learned that he was interested in cross-dressing. The mental image of him in a dress ruined it for her. This reaction is regrettable but not uncommon: "I can't have sex with you now that I know what you're thinking about."

The issue of aggressive and/or violent male sexual fantasies seems especially to inflame many people, particularly those who have difficulty with the difference between fantasy and reality. Even though many romance novels include some sort of sexual violence, the mode of expression of romance novels is so normalized in our culture, we hear few voices objecting to their violence.

Even mildly rough male sexual fantasies can be viewed with horror. A woman who is not desensitized to typical male sex fantasies probably shouldn't be told that her husband is turned on by imagining himself "pissing all over a guy and calling him a fucking faggot." When Paul shared this fantasy with Sarah, she was horrified. She couldn't get it out of her head. It kept haunting her and haunting her. "Why would he want to treat someone like that?" Had Paul merely told her he liked a fantasy involving dominance and submission, she would have been okay. But now she's not okay. His fantasy makes her think of a time when somebody beat and raped her. Despite the content of his fantasy, Paul is not at all violent or homophobic in "real life." Many nonviolent men have violent fantasies.

Second, sexual fantasies may be disturbing if they represent your man doing something romantic or sexual with someone else. Your (understandably) strong reaction might be, "Why doesn't he want to do that with me?"

Third, "wanting to know" is one thing; "needing to know" is another. In my office, when a wife insists on knowing the details of her husband's fantasies, I often work with her to discover why it seems so important. A couple should know what each person is doing in general: He's looking at porn; she's reading romance novels. But if one partner needs to look over the other's shoulder, I always ask why. What's that about? What will that do for you? What do you fear? What do you need?

My concern is that obsessing over the details of your partner's fantasies will distract you from your real issues. You might put all kinds of wrong meanings in these details, and then it might become a problem between the two of you, when you would do better to focus on your relationship needs. Think about what you would like in reality, not what your partner likes to daydream about.

A couple can, of course, decide to share the details of their sexual fantasies with each other in a more lighthearted mood, out of interest or amusement, and not need.

SECRECY VERSUS PRIVACY

A man or woman keeping secrets from his or her partner is "bad," but some privacy is "good." How do you determine what's a secret and what's private?

You should be told in general terms what your partner is doing, but it might be best to keep the details private. He might say, "I'm looking at porn. I unwind with it almost every night after you've gone to bed. I have my favorite selections, but I'd rather not tell you the details." That's privacy, not secrecy.

Of course, you can ask for more, but it's not appropriate to *demand* that your partner tell you everything that's going on in his or her head. You can ask questions about *behavior*. You might ask, "What do you look at? Do you masturbate? How long do you look? Would you show me what you like?" Your partner might choose to answer everything and show everything, but on the other hand it should be okay to draw the curtain of privacy, too.

For many people, it is necessary, or at least beneficial, to have their own private place to go sexually, where they know they won't be criticized or judged, a place to relax and zone out on fantasy. It's healthy. It's normal. You like Chinese food. I don't. I like Italian food. You don't. I go to Chinese restaurants. You go to Italian. I get a chance to satisfy my own taste buds. My taste buds are not yours. A husband shouldn't have a secret sex life, but he is due some privacy, and the same goes for you.

PORN

Fifty Shades of Grey is porn. Many romance novels, generally consumed by women and not men, are porn. Porn is about sex/romance fantasies. Unless the porn user is compulsive, I generally do not believe porn in itself is a problem. When I counsel couples, I strongly urge the partners not to try to police the sexual fantasies of one another.

Men and women are similar in many ways. They eat food. They comb their hair. They worry about growing older. However, men's and women's sexual fantasies differ. In general, they differ extremely. Of course, not all men or all women have the same kinds of sexual fantasies, so I am speaking here in generalities to which there are many exceptions. Still, it is worth noting that, in general, romance novels are boring to men, and male porn is frightening to women. For this reason, I often encourage my clients to share their fantasies with their partners only in general terms and for specific purposes.

> In general, romance novels are boring to men, and male porn is frightening to women.

Many sexual fantasies are harmless as fantasies but should never be acted out. Here, for some people, is an enormous gulf. A daydream about a bank robbery is not a bank robbery. Bank robbers no doubt fantasize about robbing banks, but most people with fantasies do not act them out. Now, substitute "rape" for "bank robbery." If someone looks at porn on Monday and commits a crime based on the porn on Tuesday, I do not believe the porn caused the crime. I believe the crime was going to happen anyway. Crime is bad. I do not advocate crime.

One of the most contentious sexual issues a couple can face that does not involve contact with other people is the issue of porn, fantasies, and masturbation. Some of my female clients have insisted that their men never look at porn. They don't want them to masturbate or have fantasies about other women. If a wife really believes her man never looks at porn or fantasizes about other women, then she's not in reality.

Men who agree not to look at porn, fantasize, or masturbate are lying to make peace. If a wife would rather not see her husband's porn or is concerned that their children might see it, then precautions can be taken, boundaries put in place, without insisting that he never look at porn again. If she feels he is watching porn when he should be doing something else, then perhaps the issue is the time he is taking away from her and the family. If he is compulsive—and some men definitely do have serious problems with compulsivity around Internet porn—then this should be dealt with in a therapeutic setting. The point is to request boundaries on *behavior*, not on what's going on in a person's head.

EXPLORING THE WORLD OF MALE SEX FANTASIES

Going into male fantasyland is not necessary for a successful and loving relationship with a man, but if going there is your choice, then I recommend a course of desensitization, especially so that you can come to understand that *your* man's fantasies are not so different from other men's fantasies.

Jill is newly divorced. The other day she was telling me about "dick pics" from the man she's dating. "That guy sent me some last night," she e-mailed me. "He's telling me to send him pictures of my breasts and pussy." And she proceeded to do just that. She was doing it only because it turned him on; she thought it was silly. What you do and don't do to please your partner is a line only you can draw. I caution all my clients about being talked into doing things they may regret later.

THE SHOCK OF WHAT HE LIKES

When I lecture on the topic of male and female fantasies, everybody agrees that men's sexuality tends to be very different from women's. Women agree; men agree. A guy could like (or like to fantasize about) anal sex. He's imagining men and he's imagining women, and it has nothing to do with his orientation. The raw act itself is the turn-on. He might be looking at all kinds of porn: soft porn and crude porn and dirty porn and nasty porn. A woman sees all of this in her man's collection, and she's blown away. *What does it all mean?*, she wonders, as if it has some horrifying meaning, but it doesn't. It's just sex.

I'm putting aside right now the issue of how a gay man's sexuality expresses itself in contrast to a straight man's. The content of fantasies and behaviors differs widely, but the fantasies of men of either orientation are similar in that they tend to be more raw than romantic. That said, I am focusing mostly here on the varieties of straight men's sex fantasies I've encountered in my practice.

If a woman starts questioning a man about his sexuality, or if she finds his favorite porn sites, she will be entering into masculine sexual territory, and anything might come up: not just raw heterosexual sex, not just gay sex, but also a variety of fixations and kinks. One psychologist counted 547 categories of kinks (see Wikipedia, "List of paraphilias"). A woman might say to me about her husband's fixation on asses, "He likes body parts? I don't get it. Why would he like body parts?" Or maybe, "Why does he like porn that features a man choking someone? What's that all about? Does that mean he's a homicidal maniac?" No. He's not. Bizarre fantasies are common for men who do not commit criminal acts and do not want to commit criminal acts. Even some women have these kinds of fantasies.

I had a classmate in my sexology program who was certain her husband never looked at porn.

"He doesn't need to," she told me.

"Ask him," I said. "Are you up for his answer?"

"Yes, of course I'm up for his answer," she told me. "I'm sure it will be *no*, but if it's *yes*, I don't care."

Understand, this woman's marriage was really good. Everything was fine at home, but when she asked her husband about porn, he said, "Oh, yeah. I can show you what I like if you want to see it."

She told me the next day. She was very surprised. And remember, this woman was sophisticated about sex. She was in a sexology program!

> "The power of fantasy lies in the capacity to explore, without restriction, the inner recesses and outer limits of our psyche. For many, it is enough to have the imaginary encounter, and it need never be breathed to another soul."*
>
> *Mollena Williams, "Be Careful Not to Criminalize Fantasies," *New York Times*, March 5, 2013.

A RAPE FANTASY IS NOT AN IMAGINED RAPE

I feel I must give one more reminder of the difference between a sex fantasy and the reality that it reflects. When we talk about a "rape fantasy," we do not mean that someone is imagining or enacting a real rape. In a real rape someone is forced, beaten up, injured. Police and judges and prisons follow. No rape fantasy includes the busted lip, the hospital, the police report. A rape fantasy is not merely a sanitized rape. It is a rape turned on its head. It is an alternative-reality rape in which nobody is hurt and everybody ends up happy. In that respect, it is nothing like a real rape.

> A rape fantasy is not merely a sanitized rape. It is a rape turned on its head. It is an alternative-reality rape in which nobody is hurt and everybody ends up happy. In that respect, it is nothing like a real rape.

Thus it is for many "violent" sex fantasies. Mock-violent sex fantasies often function to heal violence from the past by reworking it to have a happy ending. If a person cannot distinguish this transformation of reality into sex fantasy, then that person is going to be perpetually confused.

HOW GROSS WILL HIS FANTASIES GET?

Returning to the main focus of this chapter, I have the modest goal of helping a woman be prepared to learn what fantasies interest her man. Chapters 11, 12, and 13 deal with why he's interested—the relationship of his childhood to his core sexual scripts, how his orientation affects his sexual perspectives—and chapter 15 is about setting boundaries on sexual *behavior*. This chapter is about *fantasies*.

A woman can desensitize herself to male sex fantasies by seeking out personal ads on Craigslist, various newspapers, Yahoo groups, and anywhere else that contains personal ads. She can look at any section where men are looking for sex to see some shockingly unromantic and (perhaps) unappealing advertisements, such as "Come do me on my lunch hour while my wife is at work," "Fill my mouth," "Worship my big dick," and so on. Many men like this sort of direct, unsentimental appeal to raw sexuality. After she has desensitized herself by reading some of these, she might decide to share some with her man, especially if he is timid, to let him know she is not going to overreact if he wants to talk in a similar way. Her boldness may stimulate honest sharing from him. Of course, if she finds herself freaking out during her explorations, then she might need to deal with her strong reactions in therapy before going further with her man.

Another way a woman can explore is to check out some porn. Websites such as clips4sale.com and xtube.com offer free snippets of a variety of sexual activities. She might be selective depending on what she suspects or knows is particularly interesting to her man. For example, she could check out some gay man-on-man action. She could check out some kinky stuff. Fetlife.com offers a variety of this kind of material. Of course, she could just Google "porn." She will find stories. She will find pictures. She will find videos. And the "previews" are free.

* * *

After all the therapy, the talk, and the insights, eventually the couple needs to find a way to move forward. In the next chapter, we consider an exercise I've found very useful: developing a written agreement about sexual boundaries.

15

WRITING IT DOWN

A Joint Agreement about Sexual Boundaries

Who sets the boundaries on sexual behaviour?

—Sara Hinchliffe[1]

I think it is a mistake to "assume trust," and we should insist instead that trust be earned. But first, we need to think about making clear the agreement that defines the trust. Write it down. Revise it periodically, as needed. With a clear enough agreement, we can justifiably earn or lose the trust of our partner.

In this chapter, we are looking only at sexual boundaries rather than a more general marriage contract. (See Tammy Nelson's *The New Monogamy: Redefining Your Relationship after Infidelity*[2] for a good discussion of more general explicit marriage agreements.) With this focus, we will see how to put together an agreement that will be the basis for establishing "earned trust" within the relationship. The clarity of such an agreement is essential to moving on.

There should be different agreements for each of the two phases of recovery. Phase 1 occurs while the shock of betrayal, as described in chapter 10, is still predominant. Phase 2 is the calmer period that follows. Let's say roughly that phase 1 will last six months to two years; after that is phase 2, which hopefully will last for many years. One way to look at this is that phase 1 focuses on reestablishing basic trust. Phase 2 assumes that a certain level of trust has been attained, even while trust deepens over the years. In the following we refer to these phases as necessary, although many elements of the sexual boundaries agreement will be the same for both phases.

YOU KNOW WHAT I MEAN

"You know what I mean" can be very destructive for relationships. It goes along with the phrase, usually not spoken explicitly, "I shouldn't have to tell you what I want." Being vague about what you want but still expecting to get it can destroy a marriage, especially when sex is the issue *not* being talked about.

> Being vague about what you want but still expecting to get it can destroy a marriage.

By now, you understand the trouble that caused you to buy this book. Your husband has at least begun the therapy that will give him mastery over his sexual choices. For example, if he was compulsively seeing men for sex because of a trauma in childhood, he's done enough therapy so that his urges are no longer compulsions. Now you need to "get back to normal."

Well, not exactly. You need to get back to *better* than you were before. Your relationship has changed permanently. It can get better than it ever was, but it can't "go back to normal." In this chapter, you will learn exactly what you need to do to make things better.

Here, you will learn how to write down what you expect around sexual behavior. My minimal recommendation for couples who have come to see me with the sort of problems we've been considering in this book is that they discuss and write down an agreement around the behaviors that brought them to therapy.

The agreement will make explicit both partners' expectations, what they agree to do and not to do, what is and is not allowed, and what safeguards will be put in place to help reassure each other that the problems that occurred in the past are less likely to reoccur.

For example, you might agree that your husband may watch porn from time to time, but you don't want to watch it with him or know the details of what he's watching. You can agree to that without knowing more.

We've already considered in chapter 14 reasons why you might not want to know more.

The process of developing a sexual boundaries agreement should not be entered into until the work of chapters 10 and 11 has begun. The storm may not have passed, but the winds should have begun to die down. Ideally, some clarity and mastery have been established.

FACILITATING NEGOTIATIONS THROUGH IMAGO RELATIONSHIP THERAPY

It can be very difficult to go from "you know what I mean" to "here is what I need." Yet, negotiating a sexual boundaries agreement requires this kind of undefensive clarity and willingness to risk rejection. Imago relationship therapy (IRT), which was developed by Dr. Harville Hendrix in the 1980s and is one of my specialties, includes a process for a couple to clear a channel to such sharing.

Imago is the Latin word for "image." Each of us possesses an imago from both the positive and negative traits of our mother, father, and any other primary caretaker we had growing up. It is the negative traits of the dominant parent—the one who affected us the most—that will tend to interfere with a relationship.

When differences surface and one partner asks for change, the requests can feel critical and threatening to the other partner, who hears, "You don't like me the way I am, just like no one liked me the way I was in my childhood." IRT helps ease this by teaching the partners to respect and honor their differences. It is not necessary to invalidate your partner's reality for you to be heard.

IRT helps couples deal with "behavior change requests" such as are contained in a typical sexual boundaries agreement. The concept in IRT is that we hire our partners to be our greatest teachers, and then we go kicking and screaming into the classroom! Yet, it turns out to be a win-win situation: one partner's behavior change request is good for both partners. Realizing this helps both be more receptive and less reactive.

IRT also normalizes the tension and difficulty that all couples go through, understanding that "power struggles" are a necessary stage for growth. Here IRT differs from many other types of marital therapy that rely on teaching new skills alone in an attempt to help couples change, perhaps by helping them negotiate their conflicts better or setting up weekly contracts for new behaviors. The skills IRT teaches are part of a larger step-by-step process with the goal of individual healing through the transformation of committed partnerships. Because our wounding occurred in our early (childhood) relationships, our healing must also occur in the context of a relationship.

IRT is designed to assist couples in gaining access to their central unconscious motivations. When these hidden hopes, fears, and longings are no longer hidden and can be communicated in the structured atmosphere of safety provided by therapy, partners begin to see one another differently, experience greater empathy toward one another, and actively take steps to create a new experience of relationship. They agree to take on a new purpose for being together—a mutual attempt to complete the uncompleted psychological tasks of childhood and commit to becoming one another's healer in the context of a conscious relationship.

IRT's main principles are:

- *People are drawn to familiar love when seeking partners, and consequently our partners reflect the positive and negative traits of our primary caretakers.* This is why people say to their partners things such as, "I feel as though I have always known you" and "It feels like we have met before."
- *We are drawn to others who can express our own traits that we have buried from our childhoods.* So, if you are playful but your family taught you that being playful was bad, you bury that trait to survive in your family. Later, you find yourself attracted to playful individuals. This is why people say to their partners, "You complete me." They have found a missing part of themselves in their partners.
- *Incompatibility is grounds for a relationship.* Except for domestic violence and untreated addictions, IRT asserts that conflict is growth trying to happen. Our partners push back, creating an opportunity to learn lessons about ourselves and our relationships. In other words, our partners can be our greatest, and most healing, teachers.

Conflict is growth trying to happen.

Relationships are hard work. Learning conflict resolution techniques is essential. Couples can stop interrupting, judging, and criticizing when each individual learns how to set aside his or her reality and hear the partner's reality. They move from two monologues to a dialogue, and out of that dialogue come empathy, compromise, and mutual agreement.

I've taken the time to outline the principles of IRT to help you recognize if issue-driven communications difficulties seem to be getting in the way of negotiating your sexual boundaries agreement. If so, I recommend seeking the help of a qualified Imago relationship therapist. See *Getting The Love You Want: A Guide for Couples*[3] for a full description of the Imago approach. Although sexual issues always capture our attention, communication issues can be even more fundamental.

JENNIFER AND TOM'S AGREEMENT

Tom (in chapters 1 and 2) had been seeing Brad for sex, a compulsive reenactment of the abuse he'd suffered as a boy from his coach. It was important that he get therapy so that he could gain mastery over his sexual choices by addressing the trauma he'd suffered. He also needed to take the shame he felt and put it back on the coach where it belonged. After about six months of therapy, Tom no longer felt an overpowering urge to seek sex with men. Tom is straight, and he has no natural sexual inclination toward gay sex.

Under these circumstances, you might think "end of story." Tom is past his trauma, and now Tom and Jennifer can go back to normal. Why do they need an agreement around sexual behavior?

The first reason is to help Jennifer get over her own trauma, the trauma she experienced when she realized her husband was cheating on her. Reestablishing trust requires explicit steps by both of them, just as it would if Tom had been having an affair with a woman. Here, the agreement is for phase 1.

The second reason is that Tom's sexual fantasies about men continued. Sometimes, when therapy for sexual abuse is completed, the client is relieved of all compulsions and fantasies around the abuse. However, sexual abuse can cause severe psychological damage that can leave a residue of fantasies even after successful therapy has alleviated the more hard-to-live-with symptoms, such as compulsive sexual acting out. Tom wanted to continue to watch "gay porn" and other types of porn related to his childhood trauma. This happens in cases such as Tom's; it is not necessarily harmful, nor is it always a sign that more therapy is needed. So, for phase 2, Tom was allowed to watch porn.

> Warning: Some therapists say fantasies are a sign that therapy is needed, but often that's not true.

Research shows that deeply encoded sexual fantasies do not necessarily change once they are established. Just because a fantasy comes from abuse doesn't necessarily mean it shouldn't be enjoyed. Tom and Jennifer needed to come to peace (in particular, in their phase 2 sexual boundaries agreement) with his need to view this porn. However, they also needed to be sensitive to the possibility that if his viewing became compulsive or other symptoms reemerged, he might need to stop watching porn or return to therapy.

A third reason is generally important in phase 2, although not so much for Tom and Jennifer. A couple should clarify between them what boundaries cannot be crossed, but they should also talk about what sexual activities they'd like to explore. Often, a man or woman in a relationship is wanting something that's not happening, and the only effective way to address this is to talk about it and agree on what they might want to do about it. The woman might want a regularly scheduled romantic date; the man might want to try anal sex or BDSM. Men and women often feel enormous reluctance to talk about what they want sexually and romantically, through timidity or shame or the assumed closed-mindedness of their partners. A person typically might make one or two weak attempts to explain what he or she wants and then decide it isn't going to happen. A wife may feel she's been rejected, whereas her husband may sincerely not have understood what she wants. Of course, sometimes the rejection is immediate and emphatic. "I'm not going to do that, and don't ever ask me about it again." However, even with a more open partner, after discussion and maybe some experimentation, a wife (for example) may decide she really can't go where her husband wants to go. Then, it's appropriate for the couple to talk about alternatives for the man that allow him some latitude and don't force him to keep the kind of "sexual secrets" that can so burden a relationship.

For phase 1, Jennifer wanted more from Tom than a mere promise of monogamy. Like many betrayed wives, she wanted to be able to check on Tom and reassure herself that he was being honest. She wanted to have access to his e-mail and phone; that is, physical access and also his passwords. She also wanted him to be less free to "work late" without notice or go on vaguely defined business trips. He agreed to explain in detail to Jennifer why he needed these after-work activities and to minimize them, even to the point of (perhaps) damaging his career. He didn't like any of this, but he agreed that he owed it to Jennifer to make sacrifices to reassure her. Although I insisted that Tom continue his therapy to the point that he did not need "policing" by Jennifer to avoid acting out, Tom and I appreciated that she might need this kind of reassurance for her own peace of mind. These phase 1 arrangements were time limited. It was expected that Tom would earn Jennifer's trust over time and then regain his right to privacy. (In their case, it took two years.)

Jennifer also wanted Tom to hear her if she needed to talk about his infidelity with Brad. This is the work described in chapter 10. It wasn't enough for Tom to be "past" Brad. Jennifer had been traumatized by Tom's acting out, and she needed him to be able to hear her, if she needed to talk about it, even in phase 2. Of course, she needed to do this early after discovering his cheating, but years later sometimes wives find themselves needing to "revisit the scene of the crime," to talk and ask for details and basically deal with figments of the trauma she suffered as they resurface. Tom agreed that he would listen to Jennifer and not complain or argue.

The issue of sexual exploration didn't particularly come up between Tom and Jennifer, except around Tom's interest in Internet porn. Although he wasn't compulsive about it, Jennifer was now worried about the idea of his getting his sexual needs met except by making love to her. After I reassured her that Tom's non-compulsive use of porn was not a threat to their marriage, she agreed to allow it in phase 2, but she didn't want to know the details of what he was looking at. Later, when their son was older, she wanted their agreement to include reassurances that the "adult content" his father was looking at on the computer would not be visible to him.

SEXUAL BOUNDARIES AGREEMENT FOR
TOM AND JENNIFER

Tom and Jennifer are determined to return their relationship to love and trust. They will use the following agreement to clarify what each expects and commits to for the next six months. After that, they will sit down and talk together to decide if it needs to continue or be reworked.

Phase 1 Agreement:

1. Once a week, Jennifer will schedule with Tom a time to talk about her unresolved feelings about his extramarital sex. He agrees to listen to her respectfully. Jennifer may also share these feelings with her therapist and her close friend, Janice, but she will not talk about them with family members, social acquaintances, or business acquaintances, and she will refrain from posting about them on all social media.
2. Jennifer can have access to all of Tom's electronics and websites and phones. Tom will not delete any of his Web history. He will activate the locator on his phone. This is a part of his commitment to transparency with her.
3. Tom agrees to tell Jennifer immediately if he is feeling compulsive urges to act out sexually: for example, to contact men for sex.
4. Tom agrees to avoid Internet sex sites and porn entirely, because in the past this has triggered his compulsions.
5. Tom will read books and materials on male sexual abuse. He will use www.malesurvivor.org as a resource. Once a month, he will schedule a time with Jennifer to review what he has read and learned.
6. Tom will come home from work at agreed-upon times unless otherwise discussed.
7. Tom will share as much or as little with Jennifer about his healing process as he feels will be best for his recovery.

Phase 2 Agreement:

1. As needed, Jennifer will schedule with Tom a time to talk about her unresolved feelings about his extramarital sex. He agrees to listen to her respectfully. Jennifer may also share these feelings with her therapist and her close friend, Janice, but she will not talk

about them with family members, social acquaintances, or business acquaintances, and she will refrain from posting about them on all social media.

2. Tom agrees to tell Jennifer immediately if he is feeling compulsive urges to act out sexually; for example, to contact men for sex.
3. Tom will watch porn only on his phone or iPad and never on a shared family computer or device. Tom will check in with Jennifer once weekly to give her a general idea of what sort of porn he is looking at; for example, vanilla, domination, kinky, three-ways.
4. Tom and Jennifer will have a "romantic or sensual" date at least once a week.
5. Tom and Jennifer will from time to time talk together about various areas of sexual curiosity or interest.

HOW DO YOU START ON A SEXUAL BOUNDARIES AGREEMENT?

Many couples begin with each individual creating a numbered list of what he or she wants and doesn't want. Then they share these lists with each other. Although a good deal of discussion and consideration and even therapy may follow, eventually each listed item is either rewritten and incorporated into their joint agreement or it is dropped.

For "what you want," the statements should be positive, short, and present tense. For example, David from chapter 4 might propose, "I want to explore anal sex." This is clear. It is also a way of asking permission to do something his partner may choose to have nothing to do with.

"I want you to explore anal sex with me," of course, goes further. If "explore" seems too open ended, the statement could be something like, "I want us to learn about anal sex together."

The statements in the agreement don't have to be legalistic, but they should be as clear and exact as you and your partner need.

Positive statements about what you want are preferred, but some statements will likely tend to be negative: "I don't want you to do . . . ." With these kinds of statements, some sort of accompanying explanation of the fear or concern that motivates them can help the understanding and moderate the negativity. For example, Sherri might include in her list: "I don't want Joel to watch pornography, because I'm afraid he'll get so caught up in it he'll neglect our relationship." This is clear enough. If Joel disagrees about the neglect or that he will be "caught up," then the couple may find a compromise, limiting time and viewing places and other conditions. Perhaps in discussing this statement, Sherri will discover other fears and concerns, which she can discuss with Joel. If necessary, they can seek counseling to talk about it further. Deep therapy issues can come up as a couple goes through this exercise. A blanket statement without explanation such as "I want a porn-free house" is more difficult to negotiate but also should be the starting point for a discussion of fears and concerns.

In my experience, a therapist can help smooth the discussion. A therapist may be necessary when deep issues are emerging, as they often do.

The most difficult sorts of statements are negative and shaming: "I don't want David to explore anal sex, because it's disgusting." If David and Judith can't get a positive discussion going after this statement, then therapy may be the only route to take.

What's reasonable to propose in a sex-agreement discussion? My rule is to be clear but use as little detail as possible. If a man wants to watch porn occasionally, he can just say that. He doesn't need to go into detail about what he will watch. We considered in chapter 14 why it is sometimes good to avoid such details.

What are the dangers of talking about what you want? I suppose the biggest fear clients have shared with me is discovering they are incompatible as a couple and then they will have to separate. In my experience, this process of creating a sexual boundaries agreement is far more likely to bring a couple together, but I believe if it leads to separation, then the separation was inevitable, and talking didn't make it happen.

Another fear clients have expressed to me is that they will agree to something that makes them miserable, either "giving away the store" or committing to an activity they can't stand. I understand that concern, but these agreements are not set in stone. Typically they are renegotiated on a regular basis or when one partner requests it. The object here is clarity and enhanced honesty, not some sort of "legal" bondage.

DAVID AND JUDITH'S AGREEMENT

David and Judith's agreement is different from Tom and Jennifer's, because David wanted Judith to share his interest in anal sex. Although

David's interest wasn't pathological in any way, he was very ashamed of it and had great difficulty telling Judith what he was interested in and what he wanted. This was the focus of my therapy for them, to smooth their ability to talk about sex and negotiate about it. Of course, Judith knew something about David's "secret" by the time they entered my office, but moving from that to open sharing was a big step for them as a couple.

David and Judith's agreement is more a framework to explore and learn together than a specific list of dos and don'ts. The only specific thing in their "contract" was that they would buy and read together *Anal Pleasure and Health: A Guide for Men, Women, and Couples*[4] and *The Adventurous Couple's Guide to Strap-On Sex.*[5]

WHAT SHOULD GO IN A SEXUAL BOUNDARIES AGREEMENT? THE MUTUAL VISION

A few general categories of sexual activity might be covered by a sexual boundaries agreement. (Those for phase 1 are so noted.)

1. What "safeguards" does one partner offer the other around sexual activities? For example, special rules after cheating (for Phase 1).
2. What sexual activities will the partners learn about and perhaps explore so that they might expand the range of what they do? Example: Anal sex. What mutual activities will they not consider?
3. What "in-house" activities does one partner want permission to pursue without the other partner? Example: Porn, cross-dressing, self-administered anal. What activities will be ruled out?
4. What sexual activities that do not involve genital contact with third (or more) parties does one partner want to explore? Example: Internet-based, interactive sexual play such as live cam or sexting or Skype sessions or cuckolding scenes or S&M play parties. What will be ruled out?
5. What sexual contact outside of marriage, in other words, non-monogamy, is to be allowed? What is to be ruled out?

The written sexual boundaries agreement defines fidelity and cheating in the relationship. Items in category 1 might include such stipulations as the wife having access to her husband's phone, computer, and calendar.

Items in category 5 for non-monogamy (open relationships) can get complex; they must be detailed enough that the partners know what they are agreeing to. A commitment to monthly STD testing, for example, might be appropriate. Open marriages are still uncommon among heterosexuals. *Opening Up: A Guide to Creating and Sustaining Open Relationships*[6] and *The Ethical Slut: A Practical Guide to Polyamory, Open Relationships & Other Adventures*[7] both offer practical suggestions.

Some items in agreements will be very general rather than specific: "Porn is allowed, but don't talk to me about it" or "We're going to learn more about anal sex." Some will be detailed: See the rules for extramarital sex in Sam and Jillian's sexual boundaries agreement below.

These kinds of statements can start negotiations:

- Individual desires: "I want to . . ." For example, I want to masturbate on days when we don't have sex.
- Desires for joint activities: "I would like you to do . . . with me." For example, I'd like you to learn about BDSM with me.
- Statements against individual activities: "I don't want him/her/you to do . . ." For example, I don't want you to watch porn on the family computer. I don't want you to have sex with other people.
- Statements against joint activities: "I don't want to . . ." For example, I don't want to watch porn with you.

I generally discourage statements with the sentiment "one more time and I'm leaving." Behavior change is generally an evolution with relapses, even if the partner is doing his or her best to change. If a partner is incapable of change, doesn't want to change, or isn't trying to change, then, yes, leaving may be the only choice. But the "one more time" approach simply forces a person deeper into secrecy and lying.

I also advise against rules about what's going on in somebody's head. You can ask to modify your partner's behavior, but you shouldn't try to control his or her thoughts.

It is difficult to specify what kinds of rules are reasonable and what kinds are not. Some are unreasonable because they are too vague, too impossible to follow, or cross the line from setting boundaries to "policing." For example, I believe specifications around porn should generally not restrict the type of porn (say, gay versus straight). However, when rules make a point of including clear statements of specific concerns or fears, then the couple can consider reasonableness in terms of consequences, which I believe is the best approach.

> Possible barriers to making an agreement:
>
> - I shouldn't have to ask. He should just know (or everybody knows).
> - I'm ashamed of what I want.
> - It's none of her business.
> - It's her problem.
> - I'm too intimidated to ask. I'm afraid of retribution.
> - I hate to ask for outside help, or I hate to admit I don't know something.
>
> If one or more of these is keeping you from completing the agreement, then you may have to seek counseling.

Negotiation should include explanations that come out of, or lead to, self-knowledge. Phase 1 negotiations can be especially sensitive. When you differ with your spouse, it is best if you can talk about what is at stake for you or for the relationship. As you write down the things you want, identify where that want is coming from. Are you scared? Do you think policing him will give you mastery or control? Do you not want to know, because you want to put your head in the sand? Are you hung up on how your family of origin did or didn't address problems? Are you prepared to hear the answer to what you're asking? Do you need the details? How will that help? How might it hurt? I'd want both partners to think about these things as they talk with each other.

THE SLIPPERY SLOPE

The kinds of limitations that are appropriate for phase 2 will be different if one partner is inclined to be compulsive. For example, he or she might need to commit to attending a twelve-step group or group therapy. Moreover, people inclined to compulsions often must avoid anything likely to start them down the "slippery slope" back into the compulsion. For example, an alcoholic might skip social events that include free-flowing alcoholic beverages, someone compulsive with sex may need to choose Internet sites carefully, men who wish to forgo sex with men may have to give up gay social events, and so on.

Other "slippery slope" ideas are false, such as "if you look at gay porn, it's going to turn you gay." If a man "turns" gay, he was gay to start with.

However, not all men who have had trouble with sex are doomed to be permanently compulsive. Suppose a man has dealt with his sexual acting out through therapy, and now in phase 2 he tells his wife that he needs the outlet of porn. He assures her that he can use porn in a controlled way and this will help him remain faithful to her. I believe she should consider that he might be right and give him a chance to prove it.

AGREEMENTS FOR MIXED-ORIENTATION MARRIAGES

Jacob and Katelyn, from chapter 8, could not stay together, even though they wanted to. Jacob's gayness led him to need to lead a completely gay life. But some mixed-orientation couples can maintain their marriages. The main issues are (1) who will know the man is gay and (2) how the man will be allowed to express his gayness. See chapter 13 for a discussion of the various issues that need to be considered.

Sam, from chapter 7, was a good and devoted husband, and very committed to his family. However, his strong bisexual identity led him to ask Jillian for permission to have occasional gay sexual encounters. It was not in Sam's nature to cheat, but he didn't feel he could stay married to her unless she allowed him this latitude to be nonmonogamous.

Jillian's first reaction was "absolutely not," but Sam's integrity eventually led her to consider a nonmonogamous marriage with him. He talked with her about the boundaries he would maintain so that she and their children would remain the most important people in his life.

Many women find a nonmonogamous marriage unacceptable, and I believe that's perfectly understandable. However, Jillian trusted Sam and was willing to try to preserve their family and marriage. (I should note that some women favor non-monogamy.)

SEXUAL BOUNDARIES AGREEMENT FOR SAM AND JILLIAN

Sam and Jillian affirm that their marriage and children are the most important things in their lives. To preserve their love and their marriage, they agree to the following arrangements, which honor Sam's bisexual identity and at the same time honor their family and their eternal connection.

They use the following agreement to clarify what each expects and commits to for the next three months. After that, they will sit down and talk together to decide if it can continue or needs to be reworked.

1. Sam can engage in sex with one man per month. The man must be someone neither Sam nor Jillian knows socially or through business.
2. Sam will always engage in safe sex, and he will get tested once a month for STDs and AIDS.
3. Sam will never have sex with the same man twice.
4. Sam can engage in webcam and phone sex with anonymous men, but Jillian doesn't want to be present when it is happening or know anything about the details.
5. If Sam feels that he is having trouble maintaining the boundaries of this agreement, he will tell Jillian, and they will talk together about what is going on for him.
6. Jillian will keep Sam's bisexuality confidential from family members, social acquaintances, business acquaintances, and all social media. However, she may talk about it with her sister, Andrea, and her close friend, Cheryl.
7. Sam and Jillian will join an online bisexual support group and log in together at least once a week.

AGREEMENTS FOR SPECIAL SEXUAL INTERESTS

In chapter 3, Joel was turned on by cuckolding; and in chapter 5, Adam discovered he had a BDSM identity. Both couples struggled to find a balance between the draw of the men to kinky sex and their wives' concerns about it.

Adam negotiated with Cynthia to try to resolve their differences and save their marriage. She had been involved with him in the BDSM community, but as Adam's commitment to his BDSM identity deepened, Cynthia was deciding she wanted to get BDSM completely out of their lives. They couldn't come to any kind of common ground and eventually divorced.

Joel and Sherri together took up the challenge of making their commitment stronger. They planned to spend more time together and try out some ideas that Sherri was interested in. Joel agreed to limit his porn viewing to a few hours a week; he committed himself to stopping if it was triggering him. Also, they agreed to schedule some "romantic dates," which they hoped would help them remember how much they liked each other.

In the relevant chapters, these couples' discussions and agreements are described in detail. The key to negotiating special sexual interests is shameless discussion and reasonable compromise.

BRINGING YOU CLOSER TOGETHER

Every relationship has implied sexual boundaries. When a relationship has undergone sexual stress, it is particularly important to make the assumed sexual boundaries explicit. I think every married couple should do this. The "assumed trust" that your partner is keeping the boundaries you believe you have agreed to, but have never discussed, needs to be replaced by the "earned trust" of written-down boundaries that have been discussed, acknowledged, and reviewed on a regular basis.

It's been my experience that when a couple goes through the exercise of creating this kind of agreement, it brings them closer together.

* * *

This book began by considering the generic question "Is my husband gay, straight, or bisexual?" We've looked at that question using all of our understanding of sexuality, childhood trauma, kinks, and sexual identity. However, sometimes a straight man will become sexually involved with other men for more circumstantial or "superficial" reasons. In the next chapter, we look at some examples.

16

WHY ELSE DO STRAIGHT MEN HAVE SEX WITH MEN?

A Miscellany

Men are taught how to be men by "avoidance of femininity; restricted emotions; sex disconnected from intimacy; pursuit of achievement and status; self-reliance; strength and aggression; and homophobia."

—Levant and Kopecky[1]

We've already seen at least one situation in which a straight man might be drawn to have sex with men: namely, the homosexual-behavioral imprinting shown in Tom's behavior in chapters 1 and 2. We've also looked at various cases in which straight men have engaged in sexual behaviors that might be mistaken for gay sex: namely, Joel, David, and Adam in chapters 3, 4, and 5, respectively; George, Jeff, and Jimmy in chapter 11; and Eddie and Tyler in chapter 12. We've also considered a man who worries obsessively about being gay, even though he isn't (Carlos in chapter 6), a bisexual husband (Sam in chapter 7), and a gay husband (Jacob in chapter 8).

In this chapter, we consider some situations in which straight men will have sex with men, or at least place themselves in sexual situations with men. The main point is that some straight men have sex with men without being in the grip of any particular compulsion or pathology. And without being gay or bisexual.[2]

IF YOU ADORE ME, I'M YOURS

I had a client, Peter, who was going through a pretty serious midlife crisis. Peter's wife wasn't very supportive; she just kidded him about getting a sports car and a mistress, which he hadn't done and wasn't planning to do. He turned instead to bodybuilding. He put his heart and soul, spare time and energy into it, and after a few years he had a body other people noticed.

Women weren't giving him too much attention, but men were frankly admiring. "How do you get your body like that? I wish my body were like that." And Peter loved all this admiration, all this interest that he didn't get from his wife. He tried to get it from her, but she was more into mildly ridiculing his bodybuilding efforts. Maybe she felt that in a secure relationship, she shouldn't have to compliment him. I never met her, and Peter was never clear about what might have been going on for her.

In any case, he was definitely enjoying all the praise he got outside of home. Some of it came from gay guys, who were not inhibited about saying things such as, "Hey, I'd like to appreciate that body. Here are some ways I'd like to appreciate it . . ." Peter didn't care that their adoration was being sexualized, and he brushed off requests for private meetings. He just loved the praise. Being "blessed" by other men really built up his self-esteem.

Somebody said to him, "Did you ever hear about these gay apps? God, you put your body on there, I'm telling you, guys will go crazy."

He said, "No, no, I would never do that."

But one night he started thinking about it. He went to an app. He took a picture, and when he uploaded it, he got all these pings from guys, such as, "Hey that's a great body. I want to get some of that."

He wasn't turned on by the thought of having sex with these men, but he was turned on by how much they were attracted to him and telling him how hot he was. Nothing like that had ever happened to him before.

The gay sexual response generated the admiration he loved, but he was not having a gay sexual experience. It was the praise he wanted.

But Peter's story isn't over. He started going to gay bars, not to have sex with men but to be adored and worshipped. He saw other guys with their shirts off, and he took off his shirt, too. He got lots of appreciation. Peter even let gay guys touch him.

"You want to touch me?"

"Yeah," and they touched him.

"You like that?"

"Yep."

Here we have a scene where the gay men are appreciating Peter in a sexual way, but for him it's not sexual, and the physical contact goes no further than I've just described.

So, we'll leave Peter there in that gay bar being admired with his shirt off. If someone glanced in the room, they might feel certain Peter is gay. But he isn't. He is not gay or bisexual, and, therefore, he will not feel drawn to have sex with any of his admirers. Here, orientation definitely matters in terms of behavior. But his straight orientation doesn't make him immune to being adored.

MALE TENDERNESS

Women can touch, hold hands, and kiss to express closeness, intimacy, and nonsexual love with one another. They give comfort by lying in each other's arms. Women are allowed freely to touch without societal condemnation.

Yet we often stop touching little boys by the time they are eight years old and discourage them from touching each other, except for an occasional high five or towel smack. Touching and physical affection are judged to be what women do. We teach males at a young age to reject everything feminine including access to their feelings, emotions, and inner world. Gay men are the only males who have permission to be even a little bit feminine. If straight men do anything "like women," they are considered gay.

Because of our society's severe homophobia against men, men have trouble expressing physical closeness with each other. Often they feel they can't afford to act like women. They don't want to look like sissies. They don't want anyone to think they're gay.

Ironically, when men feel a need for intimacy, they often think they need sex. But sex can be difficult to negotiate with women, so these straight men sometimes end up seeking (underground) sex with men. Not out of arousal or a gay or bisexual orientation, but out of a need for tender touch, a need for intimacy. This is identified in therapy as "father hunger," a desire to be hugged and nurtured by a man, perhaps related to a lack of such nurturing in childhood. When one of these needy straight men answers a Craigslist ad for sex with a man, they're in essence willing to trade sex for what they really need—touch—without consciously knowing it.

What an ironic twist on prejudice: Homophobia causes men to sexualize their need for emotional intimacy, because they are afraid to show tenderness lest they be thought gay. Our society's taboo about female homosexuality is much less severe. Two men kissing is "disgusting" to many homophobes; nobody seems to think two women kissing is disgusting. Perhaps this lack of female homophobia explains women's permission to be physically intimate with each other without it being considered sexual.

> Homophobia sometimes causes men to sexualize their need for emotional intimacy, because they are afraid to show tenderness lest they be thought gay.

Of course, sometimes two straight men break the taboo and insist on the right to be close without sex. In the mid-nineties, as men struggled to free themselves from a rigid definition of masculinity, three words emerged—metrosexual, mancrush, and bromance—that illustrate attempts to allow straight men to "act like women" without being labeled gay.

Metrosexual mainly signifies meticulous grooming and dress. A woman might say, "My man is such a sharp dresser, and he has more brands of lotion and conditioner than I do. Is he gay?" And the defensive response would be, "Don't worry. He's just a metrosexual."

Bromance was popularized when some men decided to be open with close friendships and emotional connection. They were willing to publicly touch and show tenderness and physical affection toward each other.

Mancrush came from men who wanted to let everyone know about their adoration of certain male celebrity sports figures. Rather than saying, "I have a crush on him" or "I am in love with this man," the terms bromance and mancrush are meant to underscore that nothing gay is going on here, just two straight guys sharing a bond.

In our culture at large, however, most men cannot—or feel they cannot—be this free. Men are expected to be indifferent about their hair and their grooming and their clothes. Men can achieve physical intimacy in the camaraderie of sports or in the sublimated sexuality of fraternity hazing, but generally they have permission to touch only when they are having sex.

THE HETEROFLEXIBLE MAN

He's straight, but he would consider a male sexual partner should the opportunity arise. His main motivation is pleasure and/or adventure. He isn't gay or bisexual, even though some people might think he is. The best way to look at him is that he's between straight and bi.

"Heteroflexible" is defined by the urban dictionary as "a primarily straight individual who in certain situations can find persons of the same sex appealing."[3] Some argue that the label heteroflexible is merely a way to avoid calling someone bisexual; its use is motivated by homophobia. In my experience, some heteroflexible men do not test bisexual. (I should note that I have also met a few homoflexible men.)

When John came to see me, he was worried because he had had a "fling" with a male guest his parents had invited to the family Thanksgiving dinner. They had had wine with dinner, but John insisted they weren't drunk. Just something in the good feelings of the moment seemed to overflow onto them. They went upstairs, found an empty bedroom, and enjoyed each other. When they talked afterward, each said he was straight, that he hadn't been with a guy before, and that it had "just happened." They couldn't explain it.

I talked with John for several sessions. He confirmed that he'd never had enduring romantic or sexual interests in any man. He was straight by the beach test, had had no youthful noticing of males, was not defensively homophobic, and much preferred to wake up in the morning with a woman than a man. This same examination convinced me he was not at all bi. He also did not show any symptoms that trauma from his childhood was driving a compulsive need for sex with men. He was just a straight guy who came upon a another guy under mellow and friendly circumstances, and they seemed to naturally and easily come together. It was the situation, not anything to do with identity or sexual preference.

John is typical of the heteroflexible men I have examined. They aren't gay or bi. They have no obvious psychological issues or conditions to explain their behavior. They are men who come upon a certain man, or situation with a man, where sex occurs naturally based on the man and the situation, not out of orientation, kink, or, compulsion.

The heteroflexible perspective was reflected recently in an interview in *Out* magazine.[4] Actor Josh Hutcherson, twenty, was discussing his sexuality and admitted, "Maybe I could say right now I'm 100 percent straight. But who knows? In a f——ing year, I could meet a guy and be like, 'Whoa, I'm attracted to this person.' . . . I've met guys all the time that I'm like, 'Damn, that's a good-looking guy,' you know? I've never been, like, 'Oh, I want to kiss that guy.' I really love women. But I think defining yourself as 100 percent anything is kind of nearsighted and closed minded."

Something about the concept of heteroflexibility is elusive. No two heteroflexible men are the same. The likelihood that a heteroflexible man will hook up with another man cannot be predicted or anticipated by the man himself or by others who know him. However, one thing about these men is certain. They will never experience a coming-out process in which an inner homosexual identity surfaces. These men are straight and always will be.

When heteroflexible men are interviewed, they give a variety of reasons why they had sex with a man, including:

- It was available.
- It was easy.
- There's less talking.
- There are no strings attached.
- It's powerful.
- It's wrong and naughty.
- Guys will do nasty things that most girls won't do.
- No one will get pregnant.
- I saw it in porn.
- I was curious.
- It felt good.
- I liked it.
- It happened as a part of a group sex experience.

The phenomenon of heteroflexibility can seem like an unnecessary complication. We already recognize a continuum from straight through degrees of bisexuality to gay. (See the next section, "The Mostly Heterosexual Man.")

Why do we need something else? Human sexuality is messy, and nature is never as simple as we would like it to be. Sometimes two people can have sex, and it says very little about who they are. In particular, it says nothing about their sexual orientation or sexual identity. That's the way it is. Sometimes sex doesn't mean anything. It's just sex.

THE MOSTLY HETEROSEXUAL MAN

In their research article, "Mostly Heterosexual as a Distinct Sexual Orientation Group: A Systematic Review of the Empirical Evidence,"[5] Ritch Savin-Williams and Zhana Vrangalova identify "mostly heterosexual" as an orientation distinct from straight, bisexual, and gay. In their words, "mostly heterosexual exists as a sexual orientation distinct from two adjacent groups on a sexual continuum—exclusively heterosexual and substantially bisexual."[6] They characterize mostly heterosexual individuals as "having a small degree of same-sex sexual and/or romantic attraction and, occasionally, same-sex behavior; constituted a substantial prevalence in the population; were relatively stable in their orientation over time; and reported that this sexual identity was subjectively meaningful to them."[7]

An important result of their research was to establish the existence of more mostly heterosexual men than bisexual men or gay men. In their words, "the mostly heterosexual group usually constituted the largest nonheterosexual category."[8]

This research was picked up in a *New York Times* piece by Charles M. Blow. He writes, "Professor Savin-Williams says that his current research reveals that the fastest-growing group along the sexuality continuum are men who self-identify as 'mostly straight' as opposed to labels like 'straight,' 'gay' or 'bisexual.' They acknowledge some level of attraction to other men even as they say that they probably wouldn't act on it, but . . . the right guy, the right day, a few beers and who knows. As the professor points out, you would never have heard that in years past."[9]

In the same *Out* article that includes the interview with Josh Hutcherson, Savin-Williams is quoted: "'These [mostly heterosexual men] are the Kinsey 1s,' Savin-Williams says, meaning they fall just to the queer side of totally heterosexual on the famous [Kinsey] sliding scale of sexuality. 'Their primary object of desire is women. They're not giving that up— they're just adding to it.'"[10]

What we conclude from this research is that some men (and women) are truly bisexual but only weakly involved with same-sex sexual interactions, romances, or fantasies. A mostly heterosexual man differs from a heteroflexible man in that the latter is only circumstantially involved with men, whereas the mostly heterosexual man has a definite lifetime sexual interest in men, even if slight, independent of opportunity or circumstance.

I'M SO MAD I COULD CHOKE SOMEONE

My client, Gus, had a stressful job with a nasty boss who caused Gus to feel humiliated, hurt, and angry, but he didn't have any direct way to express these feelings. One night, he was up late looking at porn, and he started realizing he was intrigued by some of the more rough stuff: choking, face fucking, spitting, hair pulling, slapping . . . anything aggressive. Gus was so turned on, he masturbated.

Wow, he thought, *I didn't know I liked this. I don't know why, but tonight I'm really in this mood.*

He went to the Craigslist personal sections, but not much under women-seeking-men was aggressive.

Then he saw some gay porn, and lots of it was aggressive. Gus started thinking, *Do guys like this?* He went to the men-for-men section, and he found all kinds of things. "Come to my house. Fill me up and leave. Fuck my face. Treat me like a bitch. We don't even have to talk. I don't have to see your face. The door to my house is open. Come in, do it, and leave."

Gus was excited. He thought about it. *Could I do that? Should I do that? A woman would never say, "My door is open. Just come, face fuck me, and leave." Some might be out there, but how do I find them? It's going to be too hard. I don't want to pay for this. I might not want to do rough things with a woman anyway. Maybe I might want to do it to this guy.*

Gus e-mailed the man who ran the ad, and he e-mailed back. "I don't need to know who you are. You don't need to know who I am. You want to pull my hair. You want to slap me around. That's great."

And Gus thought, *I might like to do that with my wife, but she would never go for it. And she would think I'm a violent monster. It's all so complicated. I could never explain it to her.*

He went and did it with the Craigslist guy, and he enjoyed it. Not because the guy was a guy, but because meeting him for rough sex was a way Gus could get out his aggression, his emotion. Gus was amazed at how well they understood each other. *I come and rough him up a little, and I leave and never see him again. We never have to have a conversation about it. And we both enjoyed it.*

Gus kept doing this, meeting men for late-night rough sex, and eventually he felt guilty about cheating and worried about having so many anonymous contacts, so he came to see me.

I helped him understand what he was really doing, and eventually I asked him, "What about your work?" It wasn't that difficult to see what was driving his sexual acting-out behavior, but he'd never made that connection.

"Yeah," he said, "work is tough. I'm really under this guy's thumb. Every day I have to eat his shit."

I commiserated. "Well, now I see you've developed a routine to get your feelings out in the way that men understand . . . sex."

"I don't even want to have sex with these guys," Gus admitted.

"You're not the first man who's come to see me in this situation," I told him. "You discover you have feelings. You want to express them. You're not turned on by the men you're meeting, but this kind of encounter . . . it works. You've actually found an outlet for these specific feelings. That's the story. It's not related to anything deeper than that."

"I know women are out there," Gus told me, "who, when you're fucking them, want to be choked. They'll take your hands and move them to their necks and like 'go choke me.' I would love to find a woman like that. I'd love my wife to do that, but she won't. She shames me. These guys let me do that to them, and they understand."

(I need to note here that Gus wasn't talking about real choking; he was talking about pretending to choke. This "play choking" would have only a psychological effect, not a physical one.)

Despite Gus's fears about his wife's reactions, I worked with him to have some honest and coherent talks with her on what he needed sexually. "Talk to her about what you want as fantasies," I suggested. "Emphasize that it's about you, not her. Let her understand that it's an important gift you want from her and that the aggression will be playacting, with no danger to her."

I also wanted him to look at his reality. "Can we help you learn to stand up to your boss? What are the ways you can be more assertive? Is this the right job for you?" And so on in that vein.

So the emphasis of the therapy was twofold: find modes of safer sexual expression for Gus and find the appropriate nonsexual expression of his feelings.

Note that Gus was using sexual acting out to deal with his "remains of the day" feelings. In previous chapters, we've considered deeper, more long-term motivations for sexual acting out: trauma from childhood and a person's need to express kinks and figments of identity.

CUCKOLDING REVISITED

We can't say where cuckolding fantasies come from in general. Some men with these fantasies seem to have had childhoods that embedded cuckolding into their core sexual scripts, such as Joel in chapter 3. However, some of the men I've examined seem to have (unconsciously) found in cuckolding a "safe" way to explore their own homoerotic curiosity. One interpretation of the typical cuckolding scenario goes like this: When a husband finds a well-hung man for his wife to enjoy, the husband himself is enjoying vicarious sex with the man through his wife by proxy. When the husband is "forced" to be submissive and is "sissified" by the wife, this further reduces the "voluntary gayness" between the two men. The "sissy" has no choice; he must do what he's told. He is forced and feminized, which frees him to enjoy being sexual with another male. The man doing the forcing doesn't have to "feel gay" either, because the sissified cuckold isn't really a man.

GENERATION LGBTQIA AND MALE SEXUAL FLUIDITY

In 2013, the *New York Times* ran an article, "Generation LGBTQIA,"[11] about young people who are flexible sexually, rejecting the binary of labels such as straight and gay. As the article explains, "Q" can mean "questioning" or "queer." "I" is for "intersex," someone whose anatomy is not exclusively male or female. "A" stands for "ally," a friend of the cause, or it can stand for "asexual," a person who has no sexual feelings or desires.

The article considers that "identity" can be distinct from "orientation." It uses the term "fluid" for a bi-gender behavior that is "more fluid than bisexual but more specific than queer." The article notes that sexual fluidity is not controversial for women. "Some days I want to put on a dress; other days I don't." But the article claims more young men are saying, "I fall in love with the person, not the gender."

Women's fluidity has been more acknowledged by psychologists than men's, as summarized in the *New York Times* article "What Do Women Want?"[12] Sexologist Lisa Diamond has concluded after extensive research that sexual fluidity among women is common. She has summarized and developed her ideas in *Sexual Fluidity: Understanding Women's Love and Desire*.[13] Now young men are coming to be understood as more "fluid," and this is being documented in a variety of ways and is being given a variety of labels, including "mostly heterosexual" and "heteroflexible." The point of the "Generation LGBTQIA" article is that for some people the labels themselves may be suspect.

The artist iO Tillett Wright eloquently argues against rigid categories of identity and orientation in her TED talk "Fifty Shades of Gay."[14] Using herself as her key example, she suggests that sexual fluidity is more common in our society than is generally recognized and that people who have embraced their fluidity are just as human and lovable as anyone else.

The most extreme thought here is that some days you identify with one orientation, some days the other. This pushes the boundary even of what it means to be transsexual, and leads back to the idea of "fluid," in the sense of changing on a day-to-day basis.

THE MISCELLANY CONTINUES

Why else might a straight man have sex with a man? Here is a final but incomplete list of "externalities":

- Sex between men because women aren't available (schools, prisons, the military, sexually isolated environments).
- Sex with anyone when a man is drunk or high on drugs.

- Sex due to peer pressure (including hazing or youthful experiments) or to prove you're hip.
- Sex for pay, including acting in porn.

* * *

Sometimes straight men (or mostly straight men) will be drawn to have sex with men (or put themselves in sexual situations with men) because of conditions not related to kinks deeply embedded in their core sexual scripts or to childhood trauma or to sexual orientation, but only to circumstances "of the moment" or nonsexual emotional needs. Sometimes, therapy is recommended, but only when the behavior is causing trouble in the man's life. Always, I urge men in relationships to keep their partners informed and to keep their sexual boundary agreements up to date.

17

NEXT STEPS

What Do I Ask after I Ask, "Is My Husband Gay?"

Clarity is the most important thing.

—Diane von Furstenberg

The worst thing is the lying. Sexual secrets can destroy your marriage more quickly than anything done in the open. When you ask, "Is my husband gay?" you assume you are living in a house of secrets. You want to know the truth, even if you're afraid of it.

But there are complications. He may be gay or bi and not know it. He may be "acting gay," not understanding why and not wanting to talk about it. He may feel very ashamed. He may fear your reactions. He loves you and your children. He doesn't want a divorce.

In the end, this book focuses on your "sexual boundaries agreement" rather than on the question, "Is my husband gay?" This is because, whatever the answer, that should not be your final question. You should ask many more questions until you get the clarity that can lead to a restoration of trust in your marriage.

I've seen solid, successful, loving marriages maintained between a gay man and his straight wife, despite the inherent challenges for mixed-orientation marriages. On the other hand, marriages that maintain secrets are, in my experience, miserable affairs that often end badly. So I have a simple "magic formula" to fix a marriage that has been troubled by sexual issues: understand what is happening and follow up with a written sexual boundaries agreement.

In this book, we have seen that clarity leads to one of three situations: (1) Your man is gay or bi, and you must decide how to stay together or part because of it. (2) Your man is acting out a homosexual behavioral imprinting from childhood, which often fades with therapy. (3) Your man has a kink whose compulsivity may be controlling and ruining his life (and your marriage), but through therapy he can learn to manage and moderate it, even though it will never go away entirely.

Suppose your man wants to watch transsexual porn (as defined in chapter 12). That could be a horrible, shameful secret or just a routine acknowledgment that men sometimes need outlets for their kinks. If he can learn to keep boundaries on the time and money spent, and you can see that you don't have to take his kinks personally—they have nothing to do with you—then this "horrible secret" slips into a place of little importance between you. In fact, in my experience, if his shame has been making his interest compulsive, often acceptance can relieve that pressure and make managing his kink easy.

The negotiated, written-down sexual boundaries agreement described in chapter 15 is very important to a healthy relationship, because it accomplishes two critical functions. First, it brings everything out in the open, so the relationship is relieved of the toxic uncertainty associated with sexual secrets. And, second, it relieves the shame, so the compulsivity that drives out-of-control sexual behavior can be soothed and managed.

But wait! You wanted to know if your man is gay. Without the terror of homophobia clouding our vision with horrendous legal and social consequences, it is relatively easy to determine if a man is gay. He can determine it himself, using the simple tools from chapter 1: beach test, youthful noticing, and so on.

Bisexuality is more subtle. The best way to tell if your man is bisexual is to sit down with him and talk about it.

The purpose of this book has been to inform and clarify, and to make relationships easier and more successful. Whether your man is straight, gay, or bi; whether he is troubled, kinky, or weighted down by shame, you now have the tools you need to help make things better. (You may also want to seek the help of a professional who understands these situations; see the appendix.) Nobody has the right to tell you to panic and divorce. You most likely understand what you're dealing with better than anybody. You can choose for yourself. It's your future. You have options.

Appendix

HOW TO FIND A THERAPIST

It takes two to break a marriage and three to mend it.

—Brett Kahr[1]

It is not easy to find a therapist who is right for you. An excellent therapist with very strong credentials and experience might be wrong for you. Here, I will describe a systematic approach to seeking and interviewing therapists that I hope will help you avoid the pitfalls and identify someone who will be able to help you. This approach involves two parts: finding candidates and evaluating candidates. In the final section, I'll tell you about some cases in which the therapist and the client were not a good match for each other.

FINDING CANDIDATES

You are looking for trained and certified sex therapists. Here are a few ideas:

- You can find leads on the website of the American Association of Sexuality Educators, Counselors, and Therapists (aasect.org). Click on the "Locate a Professional" tab.
- You can go to the *Psychology Today* website (www. psychologytoday.com) and click on the "Find a Therapist" tab. You can also search for sex-related articles on the *Psychology Today*

site. Many of the authors are therapists who might offer you help or refer you to someone who can. Asking for referrals is always a useful way to find candidates.

- Often, for the problems described in this book, a therapist should be "kink friendly." On the website of the National Coalition for Sexual Freedom (www.ncsfreedom.org) is a "Resources Tab." Under that, a "Kink Aware Professionals Directory" tab includes tabs for "Counselors and Therapists," as well as "Life Coaches" and "Psychologists."
- You can Google "trained sex therapists."

Remember, if you live in an area where few therapists live, you can consult with a therapist via webcam or telephone.

EVALUATING CANDIDATES

Most therapists will offer a few free minutes for a phone consultation to discuss your needs and the therapist's credentials. Generally, a therapist should have degrees and a practice in counseling, social work, or psychology.

The sexual orientation of the therapist need not be an issue unless it affects your comfort level. If it feels important to you, ask. I believe a therapist should be willing to answer that question. Some people think that just because a therapist is gay, he or she should be trained and able to help you, but that's not necessarily true. Many gay therapists believe that anybody who has gay sex is gay, or at least bisexual. Therapists are not necessarily trained well just because they are gay.

In addition, the gender of the therapist does not necessarily matter, unless it is important to *you*.

The following is a list of questions to ask candidates. You're looking for "yes" answers. Depending on your particular situation, you may choose the most relevant questions or make up similar questions of your own. Some of the questions ask for the same information in different ways, and these are listed together.

1. Do you have formal training in marital or sex therapy?

2. Have you treated clients with issues related to sexual orientation? Have you treated clients in a situation similar to the one I am in?
3. Do you know the stages of coming out gay (or coming out bisexual)?
4. Is it your style to address issues that relate to childhood?
5. Have you treated clients with compulsive (sexual) behaviors?
6. Do you believe an open marriage can be a healthy marriage?
7. Have you ever had a client who was straight but had gay sex? In your professional opinion, can a straight man have sex with men?
8. In your professional opinion, do bisexuals exist?
9. Do you know about men who are "slightly gay"? Do you know about heteroflexible men?
10. Do you believe that someone can practice S&M sex (or BDSM or kinky sex) and not have a psychological problem? Are you kink friendly?

If your first meeting or phone call leaves you with a "not right" feeling, honor that feeling and don't enter therapy with that therapist. After you enter into therapy and have had four or five sessions, if the therapist hasn't set some direction, or seems to have set a wrong direction, discuss this with the therapist. Don't be afraid to challenge your therapist. If he or she won't change or work with you, then get out and try someone else.

Good luck.

WHEN THERAPY GOES BAD: SOME CAUTIONARY TALES

One day, Paul's wife, Gina, found in his belongings a bar guide from a local gay bar; then she found gay porn on his computer. She confronted him. At first he denied everything; then he came clean. He had gone to the gay bar. He had watched the porn. He didn't think he was gay, but he wasn't sure what was happening. He promised her he would never go to the bar or watch the porn again. Gina decided that would be okay. But she caught him with the porn again; he had forgotten to clear his browser history. He promised again, and then one more time he slipped. Gina had had enough. She told him he had to get therapy.

Paul and Gina consulted a sex-addiction therapist. They told her about what Paul had been doing and about his three failed attempts to stop. Paul said he had tried to resist, but he couldn't. He also admitted that watching porn went against his values, but he felt drawn to it. The therapist said that Paul's failed attempts to stop represented a "loss of control," one of the signs of sex addiction. Also, acting against your values is another sign. She told Paul and Gina that Paul was a sex addict. So Paul went to a treatment program for sex addicts, and Gina went to a support program for partners of sex addicts.

Paul did his best with the sex addiction therapy and the twelve-step groups, but every time he said, "Hi, I'm Paul and I'm a sex addict," it didn't seem right. He wasn't identifying with the stories of the others in the groups. As an addict, shouldn't all this sex addiction stuff ring a bell for him? The therapist said his problem was that he was resistant, in denial, and he had to keep attending his meetings. He didn't want to go, but . . . *Maybe she's right*, he thought. *Maybe I am being resistant.*

Finally, after six months, Paul and Gina compared notes and decided this was ridiculous. He might have a problem, but he wasn't a sex addict.

Then they went to a therapist who decided Paul was, in fact, gay. He was coming out, and he shouldn't be in denial about his orientation. It didn't feel right, but what do you say when you're feeling dependent and unhappy and your therapist tells you to get with the program? It took Paul and Gina another six months to give up on this therapist.

Paul tried other therapists. It took them four years to find me. Four years! Then I worked with them.

The worst trauma they had suffered was the sex-addiction therapy. I'm not blaming the therapist. Any of us could make such a mistake. When a client is found looking at porn, and porn is against his values, and he can't stop . . . that behavior can look like sex addiction. Yet it can be so many other things. Paul's acting out had no real longevity. A sex addict will have a pattern of acting out over years. Paul's period of going to the gay bar and watching gay porn was like a moment in time, an event, not a pattern. Yet the therapist didn't trust Paul. She assumed he was lying about his past, and she told Gina she should insist he get a polygraph test, which would force him to reveal his true history. Both Paul and Gina disagreed.

I assessed Paul. He wasn't an addict. He liked to watch porn, but many men do. He *had* promised his wife he would stop, because like many men, he just didn't want to fight with her about it. He wasn't compulsive, but he liked watching, so he hadn't tried to stop. He also wasn't coming out gay. He may have had some gay curiosity in the moment, but really nothing else was going on. He loved his wife, and all of this strife had split them apart. They hadn't had sex in four years, because she'd been convinced he was a liar and a sex maniac.

We had many sessions to repair the damage from the bad therapy. I never discovered what had been going on for Paul when he went to the gay bar, and he didn't know either. It started for him as curiosity, an interest in gay sex, and that was it.

After I had evaluated Paul, my focus changed from "him as an individual" to "them as a couple." Here were two people who needed to find their way back to each other. They would cry in almost every session with me, they were so traumatized; but over time, they got past that, and we focused on getting them to reconnect.

Eventually it was time for them to try being sexual again. I advised them to start slowly. They took showers together, lay naked together, gave each other massages. The rule at first was no intercourse, no erections, no genital sex. This slow process of sexual reawakening allowed Gina to remember how much she loved being intimate with Paul. Then she was able and willing to have sex with him again. He had always wanted to be sexual with her, so he was thrilled to have her back. They saw me for less than a year, and then they were finished. All together their "recovery" took five years, but only the last year was on the right track.

The lesson here is that when you see a therapist, what's happening for you might be confused with something else. Your curiosity might be confused with coming out gay. Your kinky sexual behavior might be confused with a sexual addiction. Many therapists are thrown by BDSM, cross-dressing, or other atypical sexual interests. Some therapists assume that "sick" sexual behaviors have to be ended through a program of renunciation and abstinence, even though the American Psychiatric Association has very clear guidelines in the *DSM-5* on the difference between kinks (paraphilias) and the psychological disorders associated with kinks (paraphilic disorders—see chapter 12). If you have trouble with abstinence, that might be taken as evidence that the behavior is "out of control." Yet abstinence is not always desirable or possible; you might actually need what you're trying to avoid. Further, a therapist might assume you've been sexually abused, that you're bisexual, or that you have one of a number of disorders. It's good to rule out things, but it's also good not to assume something is happening without consistent supporting evidence.

A well-meaning and knowledgeable therapist can make a wrong diagnosis, and the client (you) has to double-check the reasonableness of that diagnosis. Whatever the therapist tells you should eventually, if not immediately, make sense. On reflection, it should feel right. If it doesn't feel right, you need to trust yourself. The therapist can be the best in his or her field but not be the best for you.

A client, Arthur, came in recently. He had seen a therapist and told her about his gay fantasies. He had already let her know that he was married and had small children. She was horrified. "You can't ruin your family," she told him. "If this isn't that big of a deal to you, push it away." That's the worst advice she could have given him, and Arthur knew it. He knew in his gut he had something he needed to deal with. I evaluated him, and he was a pure bisexual. To have the best life for himself and his family, he would have to recognize his identity and deal with it, not deny it.

Also, it's important that a therapist not move too quickly to assume a client is gay. Ted came to see me after he had fended off a therapist who was pressuring him to admit that he was gay. He told her he thought he *might* be gay, but he didn't think he was. Then every time he said he might be in denial, she jumped on it. Every time he said something like, "Well, maybe I'm just suppressing this," she quickly agreed with him. So he knew she was fixated on the idea that he was gay, and she was pushing him in that direction. She meant well. She didn't want Ted to have to live out the pain of being a closeted gay man. But her assumption bothered him, and it turns out he wasn't gay.

I've had straight guys come in with my books for gay men[2] and say, "If I'm gay, make me gay. My therapist says I'm gay. I can't seem to get there." And often they're not gay. A therapist, on guard for denial in her clients, can sometimes assume a client is gay when something else is happening. As we've seen in this book, many other things might be involved. Sometimes a straight man will have a single gay sexual encounter, which doesn't mean anything.

If you visit a therapist, take this book with you and refer to the parts you think are most relevant to what you are dealing with. A conscientious therapist will be happy to have an informed client who wants to be an active partner in the therapeutic process.

NOTES

PREFACE

1. Charles M. Blow, "Gay? Whatever, Dude," *New York Times*, June 4, 2010.

2. Lisa Diamond, *Sexual Fluidity: Understanding Women's Love and Desire* (Cambridge: Harvard University Press, 2009).

3. Ian Kerner, *She Comes First: The Thinking Man's Guide to Pleasuring a Woman* (New York: HarperCollins, 2009).

4. Ian Kerner, personal communication.

5. Seth Stephens-Davidowitz, "How Many American Men Are Gay?" *New York Times*, September 7, 2013.

6. Harville Hendrix, *Getting the Love You Want: A Guide for Couples* (New York: Henry Holt, 2007).

I. JENNIFER'S CONUNDRUM

1. Steve Jobs, www.apple-steve.com, accessed January 28, 2014.

2. TOM'S COMPULSION

1. Michael Bader, *Arousal: The Secret Logic of Sexual Fantasies* (New York: St. Martin's Griffin, 2003), 67.

2. Kenneth M. Adams with Alexander P. Morgan, *When He's Married to Mom: How to Help Mother-Enmeshed Men Open Their Hearts to True Love and Commitment* (New York: Touchstone, 2007).

3. www.malesurvivor.org is the website of MaleSurvivor: National Organization against Male Sexual Victimization.

4. www.oprah.com/packages/sexual-abuse-resource-center.html is the website for Oprah's Sexual Abuse Resource Center.

5. Mic Hunter, *Abused Boys: The Neglected Victims of Sexual Abuse* (New York: Ballantine Books, 1991).

6. Mike Lew, *Victims No Longer: The Classic Guide for Men Recovering from Sexual Child Abuse* (New York: Harper Perennial, 2004).

7. Richard Gartner, *Betrayed as Boys: Psychodynamic Treatment of Sexually Abused Men* (New York: The Guilford Press, 2001).

8. Stephanie Carnes, *Mending a Shattered Heart: A Guide for Partners of Sex Addicts* (Carefree, AZ: Gentle Path Press, 2011).

3. AN IRRESISTIBLE HUMILIATION

1. Ada Calhoun, "You May Call It Cheating, but We Don't," *New York Times*, September 14, 2012.

2. David Ley, *Insatiable Wives: Women Who Stray and the Men Who Love Them* (New York: Rowman & Littlefield, 2012).

4. DAVID WANTS A KNOCK
ON HIS BACK DOOR

1. Charlie Glickman, "Get F*cked," http://www.charlieglickman.com/2013/09/04/get-fcked/. This post considers the virtues of anal sex. Posted September 4, 2013, accessed December 30, 2013.

2. Jack Morin, *Anal Pleasure and Health: A Guide for Men, Women, and Couples* (San Francisco: Down There Press, 2010).

3. Violet Blue, *The Adventurous Couple's Guide to Strap-On Sex* (San Francisco: Cleis Press, 2007).

5. ADAM MUST BE THE MASTER

1. Rihanna, "S&M," *Loud*, Mercury Records, 2010.

2. American Psychiatric Association, *Diagnostic and Statistical Manual of Mental Disorders, 5th Edition: DSM-5* (Arlington, VA: American Psychiatric, 2013).

3. Current thinking on this topic is summarized by sexologist Dr. Neil Cannon in doctorcannon.com/tag/bdsm/. This blog—posted February 6, 2009, and accessed December 18, 2013—notes a lack of scientific evidence linking BDSM with psychopathology. Scott A. McGreal advises caution in claiming scientific proof for or against the psychopathology of BDSM practitioners in his "BDSM, Personality and Mental Health," *Unique—Like Everybody Else*, Psychology Today blog, http://www.psychologytoday.com/blog/unique-everybody-else/201307/bdsm-personality-and-mental-health; posted July 25, 2013, accessed December 18, 2013.

6. CARLOS'S ANXIETY

1. Fred Penzel, "How Do I Know I'm Not Really Gay?" *International OCD Foundation*, ocfoundation.org/EO_HO.aspx, accessed December 24, 2013.

2. www.brainphysics.com/hocd.php reviews the characteristics of HOCD. Accessed December 18, 2013.

3. Monnica Williams, "Homosexual Anxiety: A Misunderstood Form of OCD," in *Leading-Edge Health Education Issues*, ed. Lennard V. Sebeki (New York: Nova Science, 2008), 195–205.

7. SAM WON'T CHEAT ON JILLIAN

1. Wilson Diehl, "Yes, I Really Am Bisexual. Deal with It," *New York Times*, April 25, 2013.

2. Lisa Diamond, *Sexual Fluidity: Understanding Women's Love and Desire* (Cambridge: Harvard University Press, 2009).

3. Benoit Denizet-Lewis, "The Scientific Quest to Prove—Once and For All—That Someone Can Be Truly Attracted to Both a Man and a Woman: Bisexuality Comes Out of the Closet," *New York Times Magazine*, March 23, 2014. Online as "The Scientific Quest to Prove Bisexuality Exists," posted March 20, 2014.

4. Fritz Klein, *The Bisexual Option* (Philadelphia: The Haworth Press, 1993).

5. Martin S. Weinberg, Colin J. Williams, and Douglas W. Pryor, *Dual Attraction: Understanding Bisexuality* (New York: Oxford University Press, 1995).

6. Benedict Cary, "Straight, Gay or Lying? Bisexuality Revisited," *New York Times*, July 5, 2005.

7. Denizet-Lewis, "The Scientific Quest."

8. DOES JACOB HAVE TO LEAVE KATELYN?

1. Jane Isay, "Keeping Marital Secrets Closeted," *New York Times*, November 24, 2011.

2. The Straight Spouse Network (www.straightspouse.org) provides information and support for heterosexual spouses of gay, lesbian, bisexual, or transgender partners and for mixed-orientation or trans/non-trans couples.

9. A LANDSCAPE OF IDENTITY AND DESIRE

1. Laurie Essig, "Heteroflexibility," Salon.com, www.salon.com/2000/11/15/heteroflexibility/, posted November 15, 2000, accessed January 29, 2014.

2. Alfred Charles Kinsey, Wardell B. Pomeroy, and Clyde E. Martin, *Sexual Behavior in the Human Male* (New York: W. B. Saunders, 1948).

3. Fritz Klein, *The Bisexual Option* (Philadelphia: The Haworth Press, 1993).

10. HIS SECRET SEX LIFE

1. An anonymous blog post.

2. Janice Abrams-Spring, *After the Affair: Healing the Pain and Rebuilding Trust When a Partner Has Been Unfaithful* (New York: William Morrow, 2012).

3. Stephanie Carnes, *Mending a Shattered Heart: A Guide for Partners of Sex Addicts* (Carefree, AZ: Gentle Path Press, 2011).

11. CORE SEXUAL SCRIPTS

1. Esther Perel, *Mating in Captivity: Unlocking Erotic Intelligence* (New York: Harper Perennial, 2009).

2. Michael Bader, *Arousal: The Secret Logic of Sexual Fantasies* (New York: St. Martin's Griffin, 2003), 67.

3. Jack Morin, *The Erotic Mind: Unlocking the Inner Sources of Sexual Passion and Fulfillment* (New York: Harper Perennial, 1996).

4. Janice Abrams-Spring, *After the Affair: Healing the Pain and Rebuilding Trust When a Partner Has Been Unfaithful* (New York: William Morrow, 2012).

12. ARE YOU WHAT YOU ORGASM?

1. Jack Morin, *The Erotic Mind: Unlocking the Inner Sources of Sexual Passion and Fulfillment* (New York: Harper Perennial, 1996).

2. Ogi Ogas and Sai Gaddam, *A Billion Wicked Thoughts: What the Internet Tells Us about Sexual Relationships* (New York: Plume, 2011).

3. Helen Boyd, *My Husband Betty: Love, Sex, and Life with a Crossdresser* (Berkeley, CA: Seal Press, 2009).

4. Robert Stoller, *Perversion: The Erotic Form of Hatred* (London: Karnac Books, 1986).

5. Elizabeth F. Stewart, "Hot Man on Man Action (And the Lesbians Who Love Watching It)," *In The Family*, Summer 2002.

6. www.webmd.com/sexual-conditions/guide/paraphilias-overview. This post provides a good overview of paraphilias (kinks). Accessed December 30, 2013.

7. Q. Rahman and D. J. Symeonides, "Neurodevelopmental Correlates of Paraphilic Sexual Interests in Men," *Archives of Sexual Behavior* 37(1) (2007): 166–72.

8. See note 7 above and the Wikipedia entry for "paraphilia" for more facts about paraphilias.

13. YOUR MAN IS GAY OR BISEXUAL

1. Peggy Fletcher Stack, "Should Gay Mormons Marry Women? Some Say It's an Option," *Huffington Post*, posted June 23, 2012, updated April 23, 2013, accessed January 30, 2014.

2. J. L. King and Karen Hunter, *On the Down Low: A Journey into the Lives of "Straight" Black Men Who Sleep with Men* (New York: Harmony Books, 2005).

3. Amity Pierce Buxton, *The Other Side of the Closet: The Coming-Out Crisis for Straight Spouses and Families* (New York: Turner Publishing, 1994).

4. Carol Grever and Deborah Bowman, *When Your Spouse Comes Out: A Straight Mate's Recovery Manual* (New York: Routledge, 2007).

5. Dossie Easton, *The Ethical Slut: A Practical Guide to Polyamory, Open Relationships & Other Adventures* (Berkeley, CA: Celestial Arts, 2009).

6. Tristan Taormino, *Opening Up: A Guide to Creating and Sustaining Open Relationships* (San Francisco: Cleis Press, 2008).

7. Fritz Klein, *The Bisexual Option* (Philadelphia: The Haworth Press, 1993).

8. Martin S. Weinberg, Colin J. Williams, and Douglas W. Pryor, *Dual Attraction: Understanding Bisexuality* (New York: Oxford University Press, 1995).

9. Benoit Denizet-Lewis, "The Scientific Quest to Prove—Once and for All—That Someone Can Be Truly Attracted to Both a Man and a Woman: Bisexuality Comes Out of the Closet," *New York Times Magazine*, March 23, 2014. Online as "The Scientific Quest to Prove Bisexuality Exists," posted March 20, 2014.

14. SEX FANTASIES AND SEX TALK

1. Helen Fisher, *Why We Love: The Nature and Chemistry of Romantic Love* (New York: Holt Paperbacks, 2004).

15. WRITING IT DOWN

1. Sara Hinchliffe, "Who Sets the Boundaries on Sexual Behaviour?" *Sp!ked*, www.spiked-online.com/newsite/article/11826#.Ur8897TAF8M, posted March 8, 2001, accessed December 28, 2013.

2. Tammy Nelson, *The New Monogamy: Redefining Your Relationship after Infidelity* (New York: New Harbinger, 2013).

3. Harville Hendrix, *Getting the Love You Want: A Guide for Couples* (New York: Henry Holt, 2007).

4. Jack Morin, *Anal Pleasure and Health: A Guide for Men, Women, and Couples* (San Francisco: Down There Press, 2010).

5. Violet Blue, *The Adventurous Couple's Guide to Strap-On Sex* (San Francisco: Cleis Press, 2007).

6. Tristan Taormino, *Opening Up: A Guide to Creating and Sustaining Open Relationships* (San Francisco: Cleis Press, 2008).

7. Dossie Easton, *The Ethical Slut: A Practical Guide to Polyamory, Open Relationships & Other Adventures* (Berkeley, CA: Celestial Arts, 2009).

16. WHY ELSE DO STRAIGHT MEN HAVE SEX WITH MEN?

1. Ronald F. Levant and Gini Kopecky, *Masculinity Reconstructed: Changing the Rules of Manhood—at Work, in Relationships and in Family Life* (New York: Dutton, 1995), 9.

2. Joe Kort, "Gay Guise," *Psychotherapy Networker*, July/August 2007. Available at www.psychotherapynetworker.org/component/k2/item/201-gay-guise, accessed January 31, 2014.

3. www.urbandictionary.com, accessed December 16, 2013.

4. Shana Naomi Krochmal, "Josh Hutcherson, Straight Talker," *Out*, October 9, 2013.

5. Ritch C. Savin-Williams and Zhana Vrangalova, "Mostly Heterosexual as a Distinct Sexual Orientation Group: A Systematic Review of the Empirical Evidence," *Developmental Review* 33 (2013): 58–88.

6. Ibid., 58.

7. Ibid.

8. Ibid., 71.

9. Charles M. Blow, "Gay? Whatever, Dude," *New York Times*, June 4, 2010.

10. Krochmal, "Josh Hutcherson, Straight Talker."

11. Michael Schulman, "Generation LGBTQIA," *New York Times*, January 10, 2013.

12. Daniel Bergner, "What Do Women Want?" *New York Times*, January 22, 2009.

13. Lisa Diamond, *Sexual Fluidity: Understanding Women's Love and Desire* (Cambridge: Harvard University Press, 2009).

14. iO Tillett Wright, "Fifty Shades of Gay," www.ted.com/talks/io_tillett_wright_fifty_shades_of_gay.html, posted January 2013, accessed December 18, 2013.

17. HOW TO FIND A THERAPIST

1. Brett Kahr, *Who's Been Sleeping in Your Head?* (New York: Basic Books, 2008), 6.

2. Joe Kort, *10 Smart Things Gay Men Can Do to Improve Their Lives* (New York: Alyson Books, 2003); and Joe Kort, *10 Smart Things Gay Men Can Do to Find Real Love* (New York: Alyson Books, 2006).

BIBLIOGRAPHY

BOOKS

Abrams-Spring, Janice. 2012. *After the Affair: Healing the Pain and Rebuilding Trust When a Partner Has Been Unfaithful.* New York: William Morrow.

Adams, Kenneth M., with Alexander P. Morgan. 2007. *When He's Married to Mom: How to Help Mother-Enmeshed Men Open Their Hearts to True Love and Commitment.* New York: Touchstone.

American Psychiatric Association. 2013. *Diagnostic and Statistical Manual of Mental Disorders, 5th Edition: DSM-5.* Arlington, VA: American Psychiatric.

Bader, Michael. 2003. *Arousal: The Secret Logic of Sexual Fantasies.* New York: St. Martin's Griffin.

Blue, Violet. 2007. *The Adventurous Couple's Guide to Strap-On Sex.* San Francisco: Cleis Press.

Boyd, Helen. 2009. *My Husband Betty: Love, Sex, and Life with a Crossdresser.* Berkeley, CA: Seal Press.

Buxton, Amity Pierce. 1994. *The Other Side of the Closet: The Coming-Out Crisis for Straight Spouses and Families.* New York: Turner Publishing.

Carnes, Stephanie. 2011. *Mending a Shattered Heart: A Guide for Partners of Sex Addicts.* Carefree, AZ: Gentle Path Press.

Diamond, Lisa. 2009. *Sexual Fluidity: Understanding Women's Love and Desire.* Cambridge: Harvard University Press.

Easton, Dossie. 2009. *The Ethical Slut: A Practical Guide to Polyamory, Open Relationships & Other Adventures.* Berkeley, CA: Celestial Arts.

Fisher, Helen. 2004. *Why We Love: The Nature and Chemistry of Romantic Love.* New York: Holt Paperbacks.

Gartner, Richard B. 2001. *Betrayed as Boys: Psychodynamic Treatment of Sexually Abused Men.* New York: The Guilford Press.

Grever, Carol, and Deborah Bowman. 2007. *When Your Spouse Comes Out: A Straight Mate's Recovery Manual.* New York: Routledge.

Hendrix, Harville. 2007. *Getting the Love You Want: A Guide for Couples.* New York: Henry Holt.

Hunter, Mic. 1991. *Abused Boys: The Neglected Victims of Sexual Abuse.* New York: Ballantine Books.

Kerner, Ian. 2009. *She Comes First: The Thinking Man's Guide to Pleasuring a Woman.* New York: HarperCollins.

King, J. L., and Karen Hunter. 2005. *On the Down Low: A Journey into the Lives of "Straight" Black Men Who Sleep with Men.* New York: Harmony Books.

Kinsey, Alfred Charles, Wardell B. Pomeroy, and Clyde E. Martin. 1948. *Sexual Behavior in the Human Male.* New York: W. B. Saunders.

Klein, Fritz. 1993. *The Bisexual Option.* Philadelphia: The Haworth Press.

Kort, Joe. 2003. *10 Smart Things Gay Men Can Do to Improve Their Lives.* New York: Alyson Books.

———. 2006. *10 Smart Things Gay Men Can Do to Find Real Love.* New York: Alyson Books.

———. 2008. *Gay Affirmative Therapy for the Straight Clinician: The Essential Guide.* New York: Norton.

Levant, Ronald F., and Gini Kopecky. 1995. *Masculinity Reconstructed: Changing the Rules of Manhood—at Work, in Relationships and in Family Life.* New York: Dutton.

Lew, Mike. 2004. *Victims No Longer: The Classic Guide for Men Recovering from Sexual Child Abuse.* New York: Harper Perennial.

Ley, David. 2012. *Insatiable Wives: Women Who Stray and the Men Who Love Them.* New York: Rowman & Littlefield.

Morin, Jack. 1996. *The Erotic Mind: Unlocking the Inner Sources of Sexual Passion and Fulfillment.* New York: Harper Perennial.

———. 2010. *Anal Pleasure and Health: A Guide for Men, Women, and Couples.* San Francisco: Down There Press.

Nelson, Tammy. 2013. *The New Monogamy: Redefining Your Relationship after Infidelity.* New York: New Harbinger Publications.

Ogas, Ogi, and Sai Gaddam. 2011. *A Billion Wicked Thoughts: What the Internet Tells Us about Sexual Relationships.* New York: Plume.

Perel, Esther. 2009. *Mating in Captivity: Unlocking Erotic Intelligence.* New York: Harper Perennial.

Schnarch, David. 2011. *Passionate Marriage: Keeping Love and Intimacy Alive in Committed Relationships.* New York: Beaufort Books.

Stoller, Robert. 1986. *Perversion: The Erotic Form of Hatred.* London: Karnac Books.

Taormino, Tristan. 2008. *Opening Up: A Guide to Creating and Sustaining Open Relationships.* San Francisco: Cleis Press.

Weinberg, Martin S., Colin J. Williams, and Douglas W. Pryor. 1995. *Dual Attraction: Understanding Bisexuality.* New York: Oxford University Press.

ARTICLES

Bergner, Daniel. 2009. "What Do Women Want?" *New York Times,* January 22, 2009.

Blow, Charles M. 2010. "Gay? Whatever, Dude." *New York Times,* June 4, 2010.

brainphysics.com. 2013. www.brainphysics.com/hocd.php. This site reviews the characteristics of HOCD. Accessed December 18, 2013.

Calhoun, Ada. 2012. "You May Call It Cheating, but We Don't." *New York Times,* September 14, 2012.

Cannon, Neil. 2009. doctorcannon.com/tag/bdsm/. This blog of sexologist Dr. Neil Cannon notes a lack of scientific evidence linking BDSM with psychopathology. Posted February 6, 2009, accessed December 18, 2013.

Cary, Benedict. 2005. "Straight, Gay or Lying? Bisexuality Revisited." *New York Times,* July 5, 2005.

Denizet-Lewis, Benoit. 2014. "The Scientific Quest to Prove—Once and for All—That Someone Can Be Truly Attracted to Both a Man and a Woman: Bisexuality Comes Out of the Closet." *New York Times Magazine,* March 23, 2014. Online as "The Scientific Quest to Prove Bisexuality Exists," posted March 20, 2014.

Diehl, Wilson. 2013. "Yes, I Really Am Bisexual. Deal With It." *New York Times*, April 25, 2013.

Glickman, Charlie. 2013. "Get F*cked." http://www.charlieglickman.com/2013/09/04/get-fcked/. This post considers the virtues of anal sex. Posted September 4, 2013, accessed December 30, 2013.

Hinchliffe, Sara. 2001. "Who Sets the Boundaries on Sexual Behaviour?" *Sp!ked*, www.spiked-online.com/newsite/article/11826#.Ur8897TAF8M. Posted March 8, 2001, accessed December 28, 2013.

Isay, Jane. 2011. "Keeping Marital Secrets Closeted." *New York Times*, November 24, 2011.

Kort, Joe. 2007. "Gay Guise." *Psychotherapy Networker,* July/August 2007. Available at www.psychotherapynetworker.org/component/k2/item/201-gay-guise.

Krochmal, Shana Naomi. 2013. "Josh Hutcherson, Straight Talker." *Out*, October 9, 2013.

McGreal, Scott A. 2013. "BDSM, Personality and Mental Health." *Unique—Like Everybody Else*, Psychology Today blog. http://www.psychologytoday.com/blog/unique-everybody-else/201307/bdsm-personality-and-mental-health. Posted July 25, 2013, accessed December 18, 2013.

Penzel, Fred. 2013. "How Do I Know I'm Not Really Gay?" *International OCD Foundation*, ocfoundation.org/EO_HO.aspx. Accessed December 24, 2013.

Rahman, Q., and D. J. Symeonides. 2007. "Neurodevelopmental Correlates of Paraphilic Sexual Interests in Men." *Archives of Sexual Behavior* 37(1): 166–72.

Savin-Williams, Ritch C., and Zhana Vrangalova. 2013. "Mostly Heterosexual as a Distinct Sexual Orientation Group: A Systematic Review of the Empirical Evidence." *Developmental Review* 33: 58–88.

Schulman, Michael. 2013. "Generation LGBTQIA." *New York Times*, January 10, 2013.

Stack, Peggy Fletcher. 2012. "Should Gay Mormons Marry Women? Some Say It's an Option." *Huffington Post*. Posted June 23, 2012, updated April 23, 2013, accessed January 30, 2014.

Stephens-Davidowitz, Seth. 2013. "How Many American Men Are Gay?" *New York Times*, December 7, 2013.

Stewart, Elizabeth F. 2002. "Hot Man on Man Action (And the Lesbians Who Love Watching It." *In The Family*, Summer 2002.

WebMD. 2012. www.webmd.com/sexual-conditions/guide/paraphilias-overview. This post provides good overview of paraphilias (kinks). Accessed December 30, 2013.

Weinber, Martin S., and Colin J. Williams. 2009. "Men Sexually Interested in Transwomen (MSTW): Gendered Embodiment and the Construction of Sexual Desire." *Journal of Sex Research* 47(4): 374–83.

Williams, Mollena. 2013. "Be Careful Not to Criminalize Fantasies." *New York Times*, March 5, 2013.

Williams, Monnica. 2008. "Homosexual Anxiety: A Misunderstood Form of OCD." In *Leading-Edge Health Education Issues*, edited by Lennard V. Sebeki, pp. 195–205. New York: Nova Science Publishers.

Wright, iO Tillett. 2012. "Fifty Shades of Gay." www.ted.com/talks/ io_tillett_wright_fifty_shades_of_gay.html. TED talk posted January 2013, accessed December 18, 2013.

HELPFUL ORGANIZATIONS AND THEIR WEBSITES

aasect.org. American Association of Sexuality Educators, Counselors, and Therapists. Click on the "Locate a Professional" tab.

bisexual.org. A joint project of The American Institute of Bisexuality (AIB) and the Bisexual Foundation.

www.imagorelationships.org. Imago Relationships International, specializing in therapy for couples.

www.joekort.com. Dr. Joe Kort's website.

www.malesurvivor.org. MaleSurvivor: National Organization against Male Sexual Victimization.

www.ncsfreedom.org. The National Coalition for Sexual Freedom. Under "Resources" is a "Kink Aware Professionals Directory," which includes tabs for "Counselors and Therapists," as well as "Life Coaches" and "Psychologists."

www.oprah.com/packages/sexual-abuse-resource-center.html. Oprah's Sexual Abuse Resource Center.

www.psychologytoday.com. *Psychology Today*'s website offers many resources, including articles, blogs, and "Find a Therapist."

www.sash.net. The Society for the Advancement of Sexual Health, offering support for people suffering from sexual addiction.

straightguise.com. A blog by Dr. Joe Kort on straight men who have sex with men.

www.straightspouse.org. The Straight Spouse Network, a support group for the spouses of gay people.

INDEX

Abrams-Spring, Janice, 127
abuse, childhood sexual, xv, xvi–xvii, 9,
    10, 17, 20, 20–21, 22, 24, 122, 124;
    acting out. *See* acting out childhood
    trauma; covert, 20–21, 22, 23;
    eroticizing of, xvi, 9, 10, 21, 36,
    121–122, 123; homosexual behavioral
    imprinting, 19, 24, 135, 183, 196; overt,
    20, 22, 23; resources for healing, 24,
    174; also in the spouse's background,
    116
Abused Boys, 24
acting out childhood trauma, 9, 19–20,
    21–22, 122, 123, 124, 127; addressed
    by therapy, 171; confused with gay
    behavior, 102; and reparative therapy,
    106; and shame, 36–37
Adam and Cynthia from chapter 5: BDSM,
    182
addictions, 20–21, 35. *See also* sexual
    addiction
adolescence : bisexual, 80, 104, 106; gay,
    9, 11, 80, 106
*The Adventurous Couple's Guide to Strap-
    On Sex*, 51
After the Affair, 113–114, 127
AIDS, xvi
American Association of Sexuality
    Educators, Counselors, and Therapists,
    199
American Institute of Bisexuality, The, 156

American Psychiatric Association, 144,
    199
Anal Pleasure and Health, 51
anal sex, 47, 50, 103; receiving not
    masculine, 49, 51
anxiety, 72, 74, 103
Arousal, 124
assumed trust versus earned trust, 117,
    167, 182
atypical sexual practices. *See* kinks

Bader, Michael, 13
BDSM, 54; humiliation by cross-dressing,
    140; as an identity, 61–62, 64–65,
    65–66, 103; related to crime, 62, 63;
    view of the psychological community,
    62
beach test, 8, 10, 16, 61, 84, 94, 136, 187,
    196
Betrayed As Boys, 24
Bisexual Foundation, The, 156
The Bisexual Option, 85, 106, 156
bisexuality, 84–85, 103–104, 155, 204;
    compared to straight and gay, 80, 85;
    monogamy as a choice, 80, 155
bisexuality.org, 85
Bowman, Deborah, 149
bromance, 186
bullying, 20–21
butterfly effect, the, 133
Buxton, Amity Pierce, 149